Creativity: A Very Short Introduction

VERY SHORT INTRODUCTIONS are for anyone wanting a stimulating and accessible way into a new subject. They are written by experts, and have been translated into more than 45 different languages.

The series began in 1995, and now covers a wide variety of topics in every discipline. The VSI library currently contains over 650 volumes—a Very Short Introduction to everything from Psychology and Philosophy of Science to American History and Relativity—and continues to grow in every subject area.

Very Short Introductions available now:

Available soon:

For more information visit our website

www.oup.com/vsi/

Vlad Glăveanu

CREATIVITY

A Very Short Introduction

OXFORD
UNIVERSITY PRESS

OXFORD
UNIVERSITY PRESS

Great Clarendon Street, Oxford, OX2 6DP,
United Kingdom

Oxford University Press is a department of the University of Oxford.
It furthers the University's objective of excellence in research, scholarship,
and education by publishing worldwide. Oxford is a registered trade mark of
Oxford University Press in the UK and in certain other countries

First edition published in 2021

Impression: 1

Published in the United States of America by Oxford University Press
198 Madison Avenue, New York, NY 10016, United States of America

British Library Cataloguing in Publication Data

Data available

Library of Congress Control Number: 2020949458

ISBN 978–0–19–884299–6

Printed in Great Britain by
Ashford Colour Press Ltd, Gosport, Hampshire

Contents

List of illustrations

Chapter 1
Creativity: what is it?

If a definition is supposed to offer us the exact meaning of a term, it comes as no surprise that a phenomenon as complex as creativity is intrinsically hard to define. This is mainly because it has a variety of meanings, meanings that have been added over time and are all highly contextual. People use the word 'creativity' differently in different cultures and what is creative today might not have been considered so fifty years ago (and will probably not be seen as such in fifty years' time). While creativity doesn't escape definition, the difficulty of formulating a single one does invite us to reflect on how its practice and value evolved over time in relation to societal changes. A few concrete examples may help make this point.

Prometheus, according to Greek mythology, created man from clay and stole fire from the gods to pass it to humans. For his transgression, he was punished by Zeus by being chained to a rock while a vulture ate his liver every day (if you are wondering how this is possible, note that, as a Titan, Prometheus was immortal and his liver regrew every night). He was finally freed from his terrible fate by the hero Heracles (see Figure 1).

What does this rather gruesome story have to do with creativity? First of all, the legend of Prometheus has a long echo in the Western classical tradition, offering us the image of human striving and persistence against all odds. At the same time, it is a

1. **Heracles frees Prometheus, Attic black-figure cup, *c*.500 BC, currently at the Louvre.**

reminder that the quest for a better life can have dreadful consequences for those brave enough to challenge the natural order. It is here that creativity comes in. Prometheus is, for many, the emblem of the genius, the one whose attempts to improve the human condition end in tragedy. These are tragedies that greatly inspired the Romantics centuries later (e.g. Mary Shelley gave her novel, *Frankenstein*, the subtitle 'The Modern Prometheus'). And let's not forget that fire itself is a metaphor for creativity—what Prometheus gave mankind was, symbolically, the creative spark. There is thus a price to pay for being (too) creative and creativity itself seems, from Antiquity onwards, to be a double-edged sword. On one side, an eternal fame, on the other, an eternal torment.

Fast forward to the age of the Renaissance and the cultural landscape is experiencing a major earthquake, one that has to do, again, with our understanding of creativity. While building on classical inheritance, as the name suggests, and sharing many assumptions about creative work (e.g. art as a faithful reproduction of nature), a new view of the origin of creative expression emerged. If in Antiquity and throughout the Middle Ages, the creative spark had to come from the gods (with some help from a particular Titan) or God (the only 'true' creator), Renaissance thinkers were ready to defend the unthinkable: the fact that men—and, sadly, not necessarily women—are the ones who are born with the gift of genius.

Leonardo da Vinci is a prototypical example of a great creator who was recognized as such in his own lifetime. A polymath, da Vinci made significant contributions to the fields of painting, drawing, sculpture, architecture, science, engineering, music, mathematics, literature, anatomy, geology, astronomy, cartography, palaeontology, and botany. His *Vitruvian Man*, for instance, offered the world the ideal proportions for the (male) body and stands, to this day, as one of the most significant cultural contributions of the Renaissance (see Figure 2).

It is hard to imagine another Leonardo da Vinci living nowadays for many reasons, most of them related to creativity. To start with, it is virtually impossible to have such a strong grasp of knowledge, in so many fields, due to the exponential increase in the production and transmission of information since da Vinci's time. Second, creations are children of their age and, as such, similar achievements would necessarily be judged using the cultural lens of today (a lens that owes considerably to this Italian creator himself). Last but not least, it is the ideology of creativity during the Renaissance and the admiration of individual talent and polymaths that 'allowed' da Vinci to flourish. How would he have fared in a world that prizes specialization, like the one of the last century, or the capacity to relentlessly promote oneself on social media platforms, as is often the case today?

2. *The Vitruvian Man* (*c.*1485), Venice.

Finally, let's take another jump through time. It's 2017 and Victory Square in Bucharest sees its largest protests since the fall of communism during the Romanian revolution of '89. A new generation of Romanians is mobilizing against a government that wants to decriminalize acts of bribery which amount to less than

42,000 euros (in value about 100 times the monthly wage of a skilled worker). On 5 February, in temperatures of –10 degrees Celsius, 600,000 demonstrators creatively used songs, chants, drums, puppets, masks, and even light projections on the government building to express their anger and also their hope: the hope that the *#Rezist* movement they were initiating together would change the face of Romania's politics and its future.

The creativity at the heart of this movement reflects the world of today. For example, it builds on the interconnectivity afforded by social media and it mixes and matches contemporary cultural references (as one slogan depicted in Figure 3 says, 'Make Jilava

3. Romanian demonstrators.

and Rahova great again!', where the two are well-known Romanian prisons).

Three historical examples, three different expressions of creativity, and three different universes of meanings associated with the term. The story of Prometheus focuses our attention on civilizational changes and the price creators might pay for initiating them. Leonardo da Vinci points us to the birth of the idea of genius as a property of the individual and the relocation of man from the periphery to the centre of creative expression. Last but not least, the Romanian protests—and many similar movements and 'Springs' taking place over the past decades—offer us a view of creativity as a social phenomenon, one that actively builds on online and offline interactions. Are these examples even addressing the same phenomenon? My argument is that they do but, in order to understand its many facets, we need to start from history rather than any singular, universal definition.

A potted history of creativity

Ideas about creativity are as old as humanity even if the word 'creativity', in English at least, has been documented only since the 19th century. This is because the act of creating something is a defining characteristic of human beings. Historically, our appreciation for creative individuals has waxed and waned and, at different moments in time, certain individuals, professions, or activities have been more easily recognized as creative than others. But the general fascination for what makes creative people 'stand out' and what fuels their capacity to innovate remains constant through the ages. A few landmarks of this historical trajectory, at least in the Western tradition, include:

Prehistory. The most basic inventions that define human civilization, such as the discovery of new uses for fire, the creation of hunting tools and of the wheel, the emergence of writing, the taming of animals, etc., are all part of our prehistory. It is hard to imagine how people came up with or received these inventions or what their thoughts were about those who pioneered them. What we can assume is that, most probably, improvisation and quick adaptation were considered a normal part of life. Being more creative might have given some an evolutionary advantage that came to be noticed, admired, and maybe even feared.

Antiquity. The story of Prometheus illustrates such fear of breaking the mould and upsetting the natural and divine order through one's creativity. As such, creative achievements had to be explained in ways that made them familiar and 'normal'. This is why, for example, ancient legends are full of mythological figures—including the god Apollo, the muses, and the winged horse Pegasus—that personify inspiration and talent. Some heights of creative achievement in Antiquity can be found in the areas of philosophy, leadership, and strategy, as well as the arts (e.g. theatre, sculpture).

Middle Ages. This period is traditionally associated with the suppression rather than expression of creativity. This is largely due to the fact that societies at the time tended to favour tradition and conformity over innovation, especially in the sphere of religion. And yet, there is great creativity found within tradition as the exceptional workmanship of different guilds demonstrates (e.g. the construction of cathedrals and castles that have lasted through the ages). People in medieval times believed that God was the only creator and human creativity was merely a shadow of divine creation, a gift from above.

The Renaissance. The Renaissance brought a revolution in our conception of creativity not only by defining some people as creative by nature, not by divine intervention, but also by promoting this human potential. As a consequence, creative expression flourished in the arts, in science and discovery, and, from there, in politics and society at large. Unlike medieval craftsmen, Renaissance creators were proud to identify themselves as authors and to receive patronage because of it. The allure of the genius, understood from the Renaissance onwards as an individual quality, certainly continues to this day.

Enlightenment. God as creator was finally replaced by man (and not necessarily woman...) during the age of Enlightenment. The celebration of reason went, during this period, hand in hand with the cultivation of problem-solving skills, curiosity, and empirical research. Scientific genius was especially well regarded and, indeed, many societies dedicated to the advancement of science find their origins during this time.

Romanticism. The focus on reason was soon counterbalanced by one on emotion and the unconscious with the birth of Romanticism. Achievements in the arts gained considerable appreciation and it is from this period that an enduring relation between creativity and artistic expression gained ground. With it came an interest in pathology and mental illness as the emblematic image of the mad creator was embraced by many Romantic thinkers, artists, and writers. Mary Shelley's *Frankenstein*, for instance, is a novel that fully captures the Romantic view of creative genius as tormented by its own creation.

20th century. The previous century brought with it the birth of creativity as an area of scientific study. This transition from a topic of interest for theologians and philosophers to psychologists and, later on, neuroscientists, was gradual. At the beginning of the last century, the theory of creativity was dominated by early schools such as psychoanalysis and pragmatism. The rise of behaviourism didn't much help its development, given creativity's status as a mental process. It was the cognitive revolution in the second half of the 20th century that placed creativity research on the map and infused it with a variety of topics (mostly cognitive in nature) such as ideation, divergent thinking, insight, and problem-solving. This century was also marked, in society, by radical transformations related to the two World Wars and then the Cold War—an era in which the creativity of scientists, leaders, and military men was treasured as the ultimate safeguard of victory and collective security.

21st century. The spread of computers and the Internet, social media and a highly creative meme culture, the birth of smart technology, the development of transport, and the emergence of an interconnected world have all been shaped by creative acts and all shaped, in turn, the practice and science of creativity. It is almost unimaginable today to create without the use of technology or in isolation from various (online and offline) communities. Creators and their audience are more in touch with each other than at any other time in history. The possibility of collaborating with other people, including across borders, is ever-present. Of course, this doesn't necessarily mean that we create more or better than in previous centuries. But it does mean that the geniuses of today are more 'social' and their work more 'distributed' than ever before.

The potted history above is necessarily partial. First of all, it follows the Western world and ignores the fact that other cultural spaces have their own (his)stories of creators and creations that run in parallel to or intersect those of the West. Second, it is selective in its choice of periods and trends. No historical age is unitary, and none stands separate from the others. Equally, no age had a single or even dominant conception of creativity or preferred form of creative expression. At a broader level, these conceptions are always intertwined with how people viewed life, nature, society, God(s), and themselves.

Nonetheless, if we are to find a thread within this multifaceted history, we can consider for a moment what people thought the origin of creativity was and where exactly creativity 'took place'. In this regard, it is interesting to notice that the origin of creative acts was initially external to the person and attributed to divine forms of intervention. Gradually, this influence was internalized and creative potential became the patrimony of individuals, a capacity explained in various ways, from heredity and mental illness to special personality traits and cognitive abilities. These explanations all point back towards the psychological characteristics of the person. In recent decades, this narrative was challenged by the reality of interconnectivity and expanded networks of collaboration. Even if creators—their genes, brains, and minds—remain important, creativity itself is gradually 'relocated' to the in-between spaces of interaction and co-creation.

I have referred in the past to this historical and cultural movement in terms of paradigmatic shifts: from the He to the I and, finally, the We paradigm of creativity. By paradigm what I mean here is a constellation of scientific and popular beliefs, practices, and attitudes towards creativity.

The He paradigm, in this context, designates the focus on genius-level creativity and revolutionary creations. It is an exclusive and elitist view that basically reduces creative expression to its highest achievements and relegates all else to the non-creative (or not really creative). Additionally, I use here the male third person pronoun as a way of pointing to the ideological construction of high-level creativity which consistently in history discriminated against women.

In contrast, the I paradigm is the paradigm of the creative individual. Its motto is that everyone has creative potential and that creativity can be attained through education. This is a much more 'democratic' conception even if it remains highly individualistic.

The focus on the person and his or her psychological processes has been contested in recent decades by the (re-)emergence of the We paradigm, a view of creativity as collaboration. According to this perspective, all creative products are, ultimately, co-creations and others always participate, implicitly or explicitly, in one's creative actions.

This doesn't mean to imply that the We paradigm is either the best way of understanding creativity or that it is the dominant conception today, after having eliminated genius and individual-based approaches. In fact, our view of creativity remains as complex as ever, with the added value of having to engage with the many echoes of past historical times.

The He paradigm is reflected in the continued fascination with the person of genius (Renaissance), both scientific (Enlightenment) and artistic (Romanticism). The I paradigm dominates educational discourses that build on 20th- and 21st-century advancements in our grasp of the relation between creativity and learning. Meanwhile, the We paradigm approach is highly common in organizations and society, where groupwork and social movements, like the Romanian protests, create a bridge over time to more communal forms of creating (prehistory) and lively debates about politics and democracy (Antiquity).

Definitions and assessment

Where does this long and complex history leave the definition of creativity? Well, to start with, it warns us against universal formulations that reduce the phenomenon either to an individual ability, a type of eminence, or a social configuration alone. Current conceptions need to be systemic—by considering the whole as more than the sum of its parts—and dynamic—by paying attention to the temporal dimension of creative action—in their portrayal of creativity. And they also need to be sensitive to context, both cultural and historical, in describing the nature of creative people, products, and processes.

It is all the more surprising, then, to discover that the most common definition of creativity in psychology is, in fact, simply focused on products. It tells us that creative outcomes need to reflect, on the one hand, novelty and originality and, on the other, value or appropriateness (vis-à-vis the task or issue they are dealing with).

The difference between something being novel or original is straightforward: novelty requires it to be made recently, originality assesses rarity or the 'distance' between the newly created artefact and what already exists. So, for example, a painting might be new if it is just finished, but it isn't necessarily original if its theme or technique have both been employed many times before.

Appropriateness is also easy to assess: can the new product effectively solve the problem it was meant to solve? Of course, here the difficulty is that not all creativity addresses a problem—many creative acts are more disinterested than that. And yet, they still have some kind of value for the person, at least for his or her development and well-being. For some, the meaning of value is much more economic than this and creative products are appreciated when and if they produce some kind of profit.

What about the creative process? The 'standard' definition of creativity is mute when it comes to process. As long as the outcomes being created are novel/original and valuable/ appropriate, then they must have come out of a creative process. If they are only valuable and appropriate, then probably they are too conventional to be called creative. If they are highly original but not really valuable in a practical sense, then perhaps they are bordering on the bizarre. Either way, the 'sweet spot' of creativity is hard to reach and the processes leading to it remain almost as mysterious as they were for those living in Antiquity.

However, decades of scientific research into creativity give us some clues. We know, for instance, that the cognitive processes that underpin creative production have something to do with divergent thinking or ideation, when we generate many possible solutions rather than single, best-fitting answers. Cognitively, combinatorial processes play a great role in creative production. It is rightfully said that, from this perspective, creativity operates by combining existing elements in new and surprising ways. Last but not least, there is also the issue of insight—the Aha! moment associated from early on with being creative. Altogether, a cognitive definition of this phenomenon (see also Chapter 4) would suggest, therefore, that what we are dealing with is the generative production of associations between ideas that transform the person's understanding of the world.

But cognition is not the only process that matters when it comes to creativity. Other psychological functions like motivation and emotion certainly play a role. It is long been proposed, for instance, that intrinsic motivation—or doing something for the pleasure of that activity and not for other, external gains—plays a big part in the creative process. Things are a bit more complex when it comes to affect given that positive and negative emotions can both foster creativity, even if in different ways.

It all depends, in the end, on the relation between person and environment and it is in this regard that new types of definitions were proposed in the 1980s. Systemic approaches to creativity define it as a phenomenon that emerges in the interplay between the individual and his or her characteristics, the social field (including the gatekeepers that validate the creative value of people and products), and the cultural field to which the new and useful artefact needs ultimately to contribute. Though this kind of approach does substantially enlarge our perspective—while not denying the role of the person—it also reduces creativity to what is socially recognized as creative.

More recent sociocultural approaches take on the challenge of thinking about the 'social' as not only an external environment for creative people, but also as the defining feature of the creative process as it takes place at the level of the person. How can moments of solitary creative activity, for instance, be considered social in nature? In those cases, I and others have argued, we are collaborating with the ideas of other people. In the end, our mind is dialogical in the sense that it conceives of the world not only from the standpoint of the person (here, the creator), but also of others. This is how a sociocultural definition of creativity considers the creative process as originating in differences of position and perspective between individuals and describes it in terms of dialogue, position exchange, and perspective taking.

There is no single, unified definition of creativity and this is certainly for the best. Instead of opting for one understanding or the other, it is better to consider each one as a facet of a complex phenomenon. The product approach helps us identify when creativity takes place and to compare creative products. Cognitive definitions tell us something about the creative person and the intra-psychological processes they engage in. Systemic and sociocultural reformulations help us consider the wider dynamic of creative expression beyond individual minds and point to the role played by the ideas of others and the broader culture.

These different definitions matter because they both guide us when it comes to measuring creativity and inform various research methods. For example, product approaches underpin experimental studies of creativity—where the level of creative expression needs to be quantified—as well as an extensive array of creativity tests that, again, aim to compare individual performance. Cognitive definitions also support testing, given that most of them study creativity as divergent thinking or insight. An example of the former is represented by the Unusual Uses Test that basically asks respondents to come up with as many ideas as possible of how they could use common objects like a brick, paperclip, or cardboard box. Tests based on insight involve solving problems that require lateral thinking or the discovery of unforeseen associations between different elements. Systemic and sociocultural approaches invite the use of interviews, observation, and case studies in creativity research. This is because qualitative methods are best equipped to capture process and context in real world settings.

In the end, there is no perfect method to study creativity either, as different methods can help answer different questions. These questions, in turn, depend on the theory and particular definition used to approach this multifaceted phenomenon, including the vocabulary we use to describe it.

An expanded vocabulary

Creativity relates to a variety of other processes with which it shares key characteristics. Chief among them is the notion of agency or, to use its main philosophical counterpart, free will. Creating something—from an idea to a thing or performance—is certainly an empowering act as (most) creative actions are intentional and they express the individuality of their initiator(s). But agentic actions don't need to end up in something being created. Agency is thus a broader category as well as a highly debated topic across centuries (think, for example, about different forms of determinism—biological, psychological, social).

Other closely related concepts are those of imagination and innovation. Imagination tends to designate a specific psychological process whereby we get to explore spheres of experience that take us away from the here and now and open up the past, the future, the possible, and even the impossible. Innovation, on the other hand, is much more practical as it generally refers to the implementation of creative ideas. Some might be tempted to consider connecting these three processes along a temporal succession of: (a) imagining certain things; (b) creating a prototype of them and, if successful, (c) expanding the production into a viable innovation. The relations here are more complicated given the fact that idea generation (what we tend to

15

think of as creativity') and idea implementation ('innovation') are in fact circular processes.

Improvisation and playfulness are also useful when thinking about creativity. We improvise when confronted with unexpected obstacles or situations for which we cannot use our typical response. This certainly sounds a lot like a description of creativity. But not all creative acts are improvisational in nature; some of them can be well planned and carefully executed, drawing on mastery rather than trial and error. Play and playfulness designate types of activity or personality characteristics respectively, and they certainly come into play (pun intended) in creative work. This is one of the reasons why, at the level of popular representations at least, children tend to be seen as a pure embodiment of creativity. This is largely due to the carefree and spontaneous or improvised nature of play but, as noted above, seriousness can and does sometimes drive creative production.

Finally, at a broader level, change and transformation are two notions often associated with creativity given that creative acts produce change and they also transform the world for the creator and his or her audiences. And yet, change can come about accidentally or due to biological maturation, not to creative impulses, and transformations might lead to novelty but they don't necessarily require originality as a criterion.

All in all, taking into account this 'expanded' vocabulary of creativity makes us aware of how important the issues discussed here are for our existence, and also that studying creativity requires interdisciplinarity (see Chapter 7). Indeed, one of the reasons we have so many creativity-related concepts is because different disciplines focus on different issues when it comes to the broad phenomenon of emergence (in many ways, the root of all the concepts discussed above). While psychologists embrace creativity and imagination, educators tend to focus on play and playfulness, philosophers on agency, anthropologists on improvisation, management and leadership scholars on innovation, and so on. Paying attention to the differences between these approaches increases the clarity of our concepts. Recognizing overlaps, on the other hand, opens us to the possibility of deeper knowledge.

Chapters 2–6 are organized around key questions when it comes to creativity. These are: who, what, how, when/where, and why. 'Who' focuses us on the agents of creativity, both individuals and groups. 'What' brings to the forefront the creative product, both material and immaterial. 'How' is the process question and, arguably, one of the most difficult of all to answer. 'When' and 'where' consider the context of creativity, including in terms of creative domains. 'Why' deals with the reasons people engage in creative activities and what they gain from them, as well as why creativity matters more generally for our lives.

And there is yet another important question that we need to ask ourselves, as people interested in creativity: where to? Why do we—and many others, from researchers to practitioners—dedicate so much time and effort to understanding the origins, processes, and effects of this process? Are there any dark sides or limitations to our interest in creativity? Is more creativity always better and is it always 'the answer'?

Chapter 2
The who of creativity

When we encounter new and original things, we tend to ask ourselves who made them. The answer to this question is usually a person, an individual we get to consider 'creative'. Unsurprisingly, then, the creator is a key focus in creativity research even if, as we will see here, it is misleading to answer the 'who' of creativity by pointing to the person alone.

There are many reasons, both psychological and cultural, why we tend to think of creativity as something people have (or not) and consider it a personal quality—a trait, a skill, even an attitude towards life. On the one hand, it is easier to locate the cause of a phenomenon inside a person and explain it in psychological terms (e.g. intentions, beliefs, abilities) than to consider the individual within his or her environment. It takes less time and effort to think of personal attributes than focus on oftentimes complex networks of collaboration, institutional contexts, and cultural values. On the other hand, we grow up with stories of individual achievement, from those of mighty leaders to maverick inventors. Societies tend, by and large, to celebrate individuals rather than groups; we see this in the way rewards are offered and in how stories praise the achievements of unique and singular protagonists.

It comes as no surprise, then, to know that our conception of creativity follows the same individualistic logic. As noted in

Chapter 1, one of the oldest images of creators is that of the genius. Since the Renaissance onwards, these are eminent individuals who single-handedly transform society and culture through their exceptional talent and creative drive. The visionary leader, the inspired discoverer, the banned artist, the mad inventor, the lone scientist—each of these offers us examples of outstanding individual talent and bravery.

It is not only the case that such great creators are considered to work alone (or to receive support from a small group of specific others), but they often have to fight the society and the culture of their time in order to create. The myth of the lone genius not only disconnects creators from their social environment, it portrays the latter as the real antagonist. After all, wasn't van Gogh driven to madness by the ridicule of his contemporaries who didn't appreciate his art or understand his vision? Wasn't Stravinsky's performance of his *Rite of Spring* booed by its first audience? Don't we always hear that young Einstein dropped out of high school because of the authoritarian style of his teachers?

These stories are selective and partial. What they generally hide is the fact that even the most marginal creators—that is, those who are rejected by the establishment of their domain or profession—still depend on a network of close collaborators for ideas and for other resources. The creative person never works completely alone and he or she is certainly not situated 'outside' of society or culture. Yes, creators often have to fight the establishment, this is undeniable, but they depend, in this process, on their relation to others and on the use of cultural tools, even when these other people and tools are less visible. Van Gogh did have his brother Theo to rely on and drew inspiration from his friendship with Gauguin and other fellow Impressionists. Stravinsky's show was legendary because he collaborated, throughout his career, with exceptional dancers, painters, and designers. Einstein might have hated high school, but he certainly found a home at different universities around the world, including in Bern, Zurich, and at Princeton.

The psychological characteristics of eminent creators attract consistently more research attention than their social networks and cultural environment. This has been the case since the very first empirical studies of creative people. Francis Galton, at the end of the 19th century, initiated this line of research by postulating that genius is overwhelmingly hereditary and that men of science should have a more vivid imagination than ordinary people. His second hypothesis failed to gain support. His first one—the hereditary basis of creativity—continues to fascinate researchers up to today, when we are witnessing a resurgence of biological studies into creativity, including neuroscience investigations of 'creative' brains.

Twentieth-century approaches followed this early legacy of 'locating' creativity within the person but mostly at a psychological level. Especially after the 1950s, numerous studies emerged that focused on the relationship between creativity and intelligence, personality, and motivation. This chapter will review some of this research while consistently pointing to the social and cultural origin of all these phenomena and their complex interplay.

A good example of the ways in which the 'who' of creativity is reduced to the person alone is offered by the discussion of mental illness. The idea that creators, especially geniuses, are touched by madness has a very long history. Indeed, in Antiquity, people believed that creators were inspired by the gods or muses and received their creation in altered states of consciousness. At times, their creative transgressions made the gods punish them, often with madness. There are many stories of brave individuals who dared to stand against society and the norms of their time only to find themselves ostracized and driven to insanity. Creativity was, after all, not only an individual gift from the gods, but also a potential curse—two facets of the same phenomenon of mental illness.

Many centuries later, it was the Romantics who cemented the association between creativity and insanity through their celebration of 'mad geniuses'. Responding to an exaggerated emphasis on logic and reason by the Enlightenment, the Romantic period witnessed an exaltation of the arts, of emotion, and of the unconscious. Madness was not a curse any more, but the very key to accessing one's creative potential and unleashing it fully. What is common between Antiquity and Romanticism is the focus on the mental state of the creator. What sets them apart is considering the origin of this state: external (gods and muses) for the former, internal (emotions and the unconscious) for the latter.

The Romantic imaginary transformed in particular our understanding of artists and their creations. It initiated a quest for 'authentic' forms of creativity, the ones that go beyond the impositions of our rational mind and against all cultural norms and values. This legacy is perfectly captured by outsider art or *art brut*, a current that promotes artistic productions made by self-taught or naive art makers, oftentimes mentally ill people, prisoners, or children. The term *art brut*, meaning raw or rough art in French, was coined by the artist Jean Dubuffet, who also collected an impressive number of artefacts within this tradition (most of which can be admired today at a dedicated museum in Lausanne; Figure 4). Dubuffet believed that it is precisely a life lived at the borders of society, untarnished by cultural assumptions, including about what art is, that leads to true creativity.

Of course, there is great value in recovering the creativity and art of marginalized people. But it is wrong to assume that the source of this creativity lies completely inside the person and that society has not only little to do with it, but actually represents its enemy. This view is problematic on several accounts. First and foremost, it nurtures the myth of the lone genius and ignores the importance of the social environment and of culture for each and every act of creative expression. In the end, outsider artists are certainly living and working outside the mainstream world of art, but not outside of society altogether. They might not have understood their own

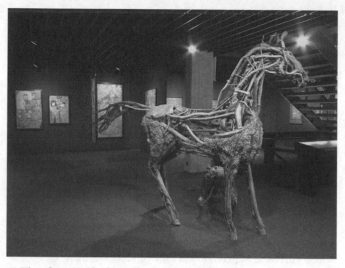

4. View from inside the *Collection de l'art brut* museum in Lausanne.

work as art, but nonetheless gave it meaning using cultural signs, symbols, and tools. Ultimately, it is because of the cultural evolution of art that their expression was 'discovered' in the first place and is now integrated into the mainstream, making room for a new avant-garde to emerge.

The story of 'who' creates will be told in this chapter with this important caveat in mind. To reiterate, it is the person who is creative, but this person is not alone. He or she creates from within a network—smaller or bigger—of relations with others and necessarily uses cultural resources, from technology to language. We need thus to expand the 'who' of creativity to include the context of the creative person: collaborators, audiences, gatekeepers, objects, spaces, and, ultimately, culture. And, with this expansion, we need to also consider the creative person as he or she develops over time, from early childhood into adulthood and old age. While the next sections focus on personal attributes (intelligence, personality, motivation), they do so in ways that view the person as more than a sum of parts— as a dynamic and evolving system that is interdependent with other systems, social and cultural.

Creativity and intelligence

Creativity is assumed to relate to intelligence given that creating involves, for most people, quick decisions and thinking outside the box. But, upon closer scrutiny, we can notice some clear differences. Highly intelligent people might be quick to come up with solutions for different problems, but these solutions aren't necessarily new or original. Thinking outside the box is not the main feature of intelligence; it might even be its opposite, given that intelligent people are particularly good at applying existing knowledge to newly found problems. Creative people, on the other hand, try other options and build new knowledge in the process. Intuitively, we all know people we consider very smart but not necessarily creative and, perhaps, the other way around. And yet, it is undeniable that creativity and intelligence do support each other. The question is how.

In many ways, creativity research grew out of research on intelligence or the intellect. The initial major concern for the first creativity researchers was to demonstrate that creativity is, indeed, different from intelligence. Having developed the first tests for both constructs, they were keen to notice whether intelligence and creativity were highly correlated (meaning that the higher a person scores on an intelligence test, the higher they would score on a creativity one). High correlations could indicate, in this context, that we are measuring the same construct or, in other words, that creativity is not the same as intelligence. Luckily for creativity researchers, they did find an interesting difference.

Creativity and intelligence do relate closely to each other up to about 120 IQ points (slightly more than the average for intelligence), but their relation is much weaker above this score.

Known as the threshold hypothesis, this finding made researchers conclude that an average level of intelligence is required for creative production, and yet, 'more' intelligence doesn't necessarily make people more creative; it neither helps nor hinders creativity.

Empirical evidence supporting or disconfirming the threshold hypothesis has been accumulating since these early days of research, and the issue is not resolved. Recent meta-analyses, using more sophisticated tools such as Necessary Condition Analysis, found that there is a necessary-but-not-sufficient relationship between intelligence and creativity and, thus, that while these two phenomena are not identical, they do overlap to some extent. This makes sense considering the fact that eminence (high IQs) is viewed as an essential condition for discovering geniuses and geniuses are, more or less, the prototype of successful creators.

At the same time, the distinction between convergent and divergent thinking, popular in creativity research, gives us a hint as to what distinguishes intelligence from creativity. The first type helps us reach one, correct solution, and it is therefore required for well-defined problems, the kind students usually deal with at school. In contrast, divergent thinking goes into many directions, all of them plausible, none of them 'correct', and it applies to ill-defined or open problems specific for everyday life. The former is central for intelligence, the latter, as suspected, a key contributor to the creative process.

But intelligence itself shouldn't be reduced to a single factor or dimension. In fact, not all intelligence researchers agree on what intelligence is. The history of studying this phenomenon reveals, in fact, some interesting debates concerning whether intelligence is a unitary process or actually a set of specific abilities. And even if we could talk about a general factor of intelligence, this can be further divided into a crystallized and fluid form, the former working deductively and the latter inductively.

One consistent critique addressed to these classifications is that they deal with a rather narrow view of intelligence that applies to school settings and focuses on logic above all else. What other things can intelligence help us accomplish? Howard Gardner famously argued that we should be talking about multiple processes that support our talents and abilities. For example, he identified eight intelligences: musical-rhythmic, visual-spatial, verbal-linguistic, logical-mathematical, bodily-kinaesthetic, interpersonal, intrapersonal, and naturalistic. Interestingly, Gardner proposed for each one of these types particular forms of genius, thus explicitly relating the expression of intelligence to that of creativity.

Robert J. Sternberg's triadic model goes even further in emphasizing this connection by directly talking about analytical, practical, and creative intelligence. The first one corresponds to the more traditional 'academic' type, the second one focuses on adapting to everyday situations, and the third one is concerned with transforming these situations creatively. Nowadays, the term emotional intelligence, or the kind of cleverness that makes us attuned to our own emotions and the emotions of others, is increasingly popular. Given that creativity is infused by a range of emotions and that it involves taking the perspective of others in an empathetic manner, new bridges between the two phenomena are being built.

In understanding the nature of the relation between intelligence and creativity it is not enough, however, to examine their sub-processes and dimensions. What we also need is to place the two in context, in particular the social, material, and cultural contexts that give birth to both. Intelligence and, to a certain extent, creativity are commonly seen as taking place 'in the head' and being features we are either born with or not. This is a highly misleading perspective, as scientific research in these areas shows not only that these phenomena are malleable, but that they can be educated given the right environmental conditions. The more we consider intelligence to be a set of abilities and talents, the more we can see that nature and nurture both contribute to its expression.

In addition, the origin of intelligent behaviour, as the developmental work of Piaget and Vygotsky reminds us, can be firmly located within interactions with objects and with other people during early childhood. The absence of such supportive interactions or lack of immersion within a cultural world of symbols, tools, and institutions deprive the person of his or her potential to act intelligently *and* creatively. Moreover, it is the pattern of these actions and interactions that should be of great importance for those who study creative people, an issue that brings us to our next topic, personality.

Creativity and personality

Personality has been a main concern for psychologists throughout the last century and personality psychology is a thriving area of research to this day. In lay terms, personality is what makes us who we are, the unique combination of traits and characteristics that distinguishes us from others. And yet, it is exactly these traits that also relate us to other people. For example, being perceptive or enthusiastic most of the time describes more than one person. It is what many individuals have in common and what can even bring them together. It is thus the original combination of personality traits, developed and expressed across the lifespan, that give us our uniqueness.

In this way, we might even consider personality development as a creative process, initially based on innate predispositions and the guidance of the environment and gradually self-directed by the person who gets to choose the types of situations and interactions that cultivate certain characteristics and not others. Each personality is finally original, at least to some extent, and its traits are meant to adapt us to the world around us, thus demonstrating value (even if specific traits might end up being un-adaptive or even border on the pathological). But can we think of creativity itself as a personality trait?

In answering this question, we have to define better what traits are. They are ways of being in the world and reacting to certain situations that have a level of stability across time and across contexts (without being inflexible). In other words, if we say about someone that he or she is determined, then we expect a certain level of determination from him or her when interacting with family members, work colleagues, and even strangers. Of course, here is where personality theory tends to receive considerable criticism, especially from social psychologists who point to the power of situations in shaping our thinking and behaviour.

For instance, we might not want to think of ourselves as acting in a cowardly or cruel way towards others, and yet we might do so, with great consistency, in given circumstances. This discussion about cross-situational stability is relevant for creativity given that, if creativity is a personality trait, then its expression should be relatively stable across contexts and domains—in the family home, at work, at the market, in mathematics, poetry, or sports. On the one hand, we could imagine someone approaching these different contexts and domains creatively but, on the other, creative expression depends on much more than personality; it requires knowledge, skills, and favourable social relations.

Recognizing this, psychologists aimed to understand which personality traits might support (or inhibit) creative behaviour in general as well as in specific domains. Decades of research into this question produced impressive lists of personality attributes correlated to creativity across domains, including playfulness, tolerance of ambiguity, preference for complexity, autonomy, flexibility, risk taking, curiosity, broad interests, independence of judgement, nonconformism, aesthetic or artistic preferences, and so on.

In fact, the list is so long that one might wonder if it is useful at all. For instance, knowing that flexibility as a personality trait relates to creativity is useful but also highly predictable. In some ways, many of the traits above don't add to our knowledge of creative people, being either too general or already part of how we understand creativity (e.g. in terms of curiosity and aesthetics). Moreover, the personality profiles of a creative artist and scientist might differ and, indeed, there is ample research available to support this claim. For example, thoroughness might not necessarily be required for creative achievement in the arts, but it emerges as a key quality for creative scientists. What do we learn, then, from studying personality and creativity together?

There is one highly popular theory, the Big Five, that can shed some light on that. The Big Five basically designates five 'super' traits that emerged from grouping, statistically, a wide range of personality characteristics, across ages and cultures. These are extraversion (whether someone is more sociable and outgoing versus reserved), neuroticism (sensitive and nervous versus confident), conscientiousness (well organized versus careless), openness to experience (inventive and curious versus cautious), and agreeableness (friendly and compassionate versus detached).

It is not hard, from the short descriptions above, to figure out which of the Big Five features relates most intimately with creativity. Yes, you guessed it, it's openness to experience. This personality trait includes several sub-dimensions such as an active imagination, attentiveness to feelings, aesthetic sensitivity, preference for variety, and intellectual curiosity. Given this description, one might question why openness to experience is not directly called 'creativity'. The answer goes back to the difference between a generally open approach to different situations (personality) and actually getting to produce things that are new, original, and useful (creativity). In fact, the latter requires the collaboration between various traits and, beyond them, the existence of knowledge, skills, and motives.

Conscientiousness, to take another example, often emerges as the opposite of creative expression given that conscientious people tend to be self-disciplined, careful, and diligent. This doesn't sound like the profile of a creative artist. But it certainly does contribute to creativity in science and other domains. And, even in art, successful creators don't only engage in messy creative processes, they also need to get themselves organized in order to promote their own work. This is where a bit of conscientiousness comes in handy.

A question that is not raised enough in research on personality and creativity is *how* exactly we get to be open to experience or conscientious. This question points us to the role of the environment, life experience, and interactions with other people in becoming who we are and, in our case, in becoming creative. Personality, just like intelligence, is not a set of 'internal' features that develop and are manifested independent of the 'outside' world. On the contrary, both personality and creativity are forged within complex networks of interaction and adapted to their context. The link between person and situation, in fact, takes us directly to our last topic, motivation. It is not the case that possessing certain traits and skills within a specific context makes us, automatically, more creative. It is how we arrived there in the first place and what we might want to do that matter most.

Creativity and motivation

Motivation answers the question of why we do what we do. In the case of creativity, this means knowing why people choose to express themselves creatively, including when, where, and in relation to what. A quick reflection on what helps us choose to be creative rather than apply conventional, tried and tested solutions, reveals a wide range of possible motives (see also Chapter 6). For example, we might create out of necessity given that we are dealing with an unusual problem for which we have no habitual answer. But we can very well enjoy taking an alternative path and discovering new solutions for an old challenge. We often choose to do things creatively because it makes us feel better. Then there are also the praise or rewards, including financial, we might get from our creativity. This can be a strong motivator. Which doesn't mean we don't still enjoy doing what we are doing.

The picture of motivation is thus complex and any simple distinction between intrinsic motivation—doing something for its own sake—and extrinsic motivation—doing things for other reasons, including to avoid punishment or get a reward—doesn't do justice to this complexity. We tend to think, at first sight, that intrinsic motivation is conducive for creativity given that really enjoying what you do is a feeling shared by a lot of creative people. This has also been repeatedly demonstrated in research, particularly by Teresa Amabile and her collaborators. So strong was the evidence that creative activities are experienced as inherently rewarding that Amabile even proposed this as the 'intrinsic motivation principle of creativity'.

Since then, however, a more nuanced understanding developed, showing that extrinsic motivation doesn't always—at all times, for all people, and in all contexts—diminish creativity. While it is true that rewarding creative behaviours that might otherwise have been done for their intrinsic benefits can reduce our tendency to engage in them (at least when the rewards we become used to are absent), we are certainly acting creatively for both intrinsic and extrinsic reasons in everyday life.

Motivation can also be discussed in terms of goals or the end states that energize and guide us in doing something. It's common to distinguish, in this regard, between mastery and learning goals, that focus on the personal benefits of the activity for the person, and performance goals, that set up standards to be achieved.

When it comes to creativity, a big drive is certainly represented by doing something in a masterful manner and learning in the process. There is always something new to discover, about ourselves or about the world, when being creative. On the other hand, we cannot dismiss the fact that, oftentimes, we also care a lot about the quality of our creative outcomes. This drive towards performance can be experienced as a 'competition with oneself', when the person wants to better his or her previous creations, or a competition with others and the standards set up by their work. This is when, for instance, external rewards such as money or recognition, come into play and can end up either motivating or demotivating creative people.

This discussion of motives and goals has practical applications for cultivating creativity from early childhood onwards. Praising children for their creative outputs, expressed in the form of beautiful drawings, amusing stories, or brilliant science projects, can have positive or negative effects on their future creativity. While positive and constructive feedback is always welcomed, if it emphasizes performance alone (e.g. 'You have done the most beautiful drawing I have ever seen') or personal qualities (e.g. 'You are the most creative little girl in the world!'), it can lead to a focus on outcome and talent at the expense of joy, learning, effort, and mastery. This will boost the self-esteem of the little creator, certainly, but in the long term it might discourage children from engaging in creative behaviour, especially if they don't feel they can be 'the best that ever was'.

The impact of what we believe about ourselves on motivation is captured by the notion of mindsets. Carol Dweck famously distinguished here between a fixed mindset, basically implying that our qualities—including intelligence and creativity—are finite and fixed at birth, and a malleable or growth one, emphasizing the flexibility of our traits and the importance of learning. It is predictable that a person with a fixed mindset about creativity won't put in much effort to improve once he or she fails at a creative task. Growth mindset people, however, will be motivated to learn and become better when being challenged. Success and failure, again, depend largely on the views and feedback of others.

It is from this discussion of motivation and social interaction that we can develop a new understanding of the importance of the environment for the most 'personal' or psychological aspects of creativity. We might imagine motives to be creative as highly individual, determined by the person alone but, in fact, just like intelligence and personality, motivation depends both on self and others, on what we bring to, and on what we receive from, our environment. The motivation to be creative originates in early life interactions with care-givers and peers, in episodes of pretend play and in the process of understanding what other people think about our creative outcomes and our abilities.

In this sense, the 'who' of creativity is much less individual than initially thought. Or, rather, individual resources for creativity—such as intelligence, specific personality traits, types of emotion and motivation—are shaped by practical action and interactions with others.

One last interesting question to raise in this chapter is why, if we all possess traits and abilities conducive for creativity, at least to some extent, more people don't express themselves creatively. This question reinforces the above: the fact that creativity doesn't depend solely on personal attributes or, for this matter, on context and circumstance alone.

In order for someone to act creatively, he or she needs, among other things, different types of intelligence, openness to experience, and some intrinsic motivation. But these individual qualities have to 'meet' an environment favourable for creative expression. If cultural norms prioritize conformity over personal initiative, if others criticize creative work or if they offer disproportionate rewards or inadequate praise, and if one's openness to the world is not matched by the world's receptiveness to the person's view and contributions, then creativity won't flourish. This interaction between person and environment will become even more obvious as we discuss, next, the nature of creative products and their reception.

Chapter 3
The what of creativity

A remarkable thing to reflect on is that everything man-made that surrounds us has been, at some point in time, a product of human creativity. The table and chairs, pencils and paper, not to mention the mobile phone or laptop, they were all invented, either thousands of years ago or a mere few decades back. There was a time when we didn't have these things, maybe we weren't even able to imagine them. And yet, someone—most probably groups or communities rather than individual creators—started making versions of them. And, in this day and age, other people continue to improve these artefacts and create new ones.

The only reason we don't recognize most things around us as creative outcomes is that we've become used to them. They are conventional, part of the everyday. It takes an effort of imagination to picture how the world was before they were created, who created them and how, and where we would be today without them. These are some of the questions we get to reflect on in this chapter.

The 'what' of creativity is represented by those products coming out of creative processes. And these products vary widely. Designer chairs, cups made of entirely new and sustainable materials, the latest version of a mobile phone, are all tangible outcomes. But ideas can also be called creative even if they are, at least at first, intangible. To complicate things further, processes can also be considered creative outcomes. Think, for example, about dance, music, or theatre performances. Creativity, in these latter cases, unfolds over time.

From the start, we should note that creativity research is primarily focused on products. This becomes clear when considering the definition of the phenomenon (see Chapter 1). Generating new and original as well as valuable outcomes is, essentially, a product definition. There are specific benefits to approaching creativity from the perspective of its outcomes. First and foremost, we can measure these productions—in terms of their novelty, originality, or appropriateness—and thus gain a clear idea of whether something creative has happened or not. Products are also available for others to evaluate and they can be, in most cases, preserved over time (e.g. a unique music performance can be recorded, the oldest pieces of paper ever to be written on can be kept in a museum, and so on).

But there is also a limit to our product focus. Most of all, we have little process information from it. So, for instance, if two people come to the same mathematical conclusion and we only evaluate this end point, we entirely miss how they solved the problem. And creative value might reside in the 'how' rather than the 'what'. We risk misjudging the creativity of less impressive outcomes in the absence of knowledge about their becoming.

In understanding the 'what' of creativity, then, we need to expand our focus and consider creative artefacts in connection to creative processes which are in turn, as we saw in Chapter 2, related to the abilities and life contexts of the creative person. More than this, we need to consider creative outcomes also in the broader context of society and history. Indeed, how would we ever be able to appreciate something as new, if we didn't know what already exists in society? Or how can something be original if it came about many times throughout history? Even value and appropriateness are contextual in nature. A solution that works for a certain person or group, at a certain point in time, might fail miserably for other people, at another time.

Every assessment of something as new, original, and useful, therefore, should specify *for whom* and *when*. This doesn't mean that creativity is completely 'in the eye of the beholder', but that the quality of being creative is based on an ongoing negotiation between creators, audiences, and the creation itself.

In the end, we need to consider culture in any analysis of creative products. It is against a specific cultural background that the outcomes of our creativity are positioned and made sense of. The new doesn't come to replace the old but is, in fact, integrated within it. It is through cultural means, including language, that we come to understand the novel outcomes and appropriate them. This process leads not only to the transformation of the old through the integration of novelty, but it also changes how we perceive the novelty itself.

One key process at play here is conventionalization. The new gradually turns into the old. But other things happen as well that contribute to further creativity. For example, cultural transmission helps creative artefacts go through different 'incarnations' as they are circulated within society. Think, for instance, about the evolution of social media and how many new forms are available today based on variations on the same basic principle of online participation. Diversification and modification are part and parcel of cultural transmission.

What is interesting to notice about cultural evolution and its relation to creativity is how creative people and outcomes tend to cluster together at different moments in history and across specific places, leading to the emergence of Golden Ages. Such periods, marked by rapid advancements in multiple fields (social, political, economic, artistic, scientific, technological, etc.), have been identified in relation to various civilizations around the world, from Greek and Roman to Aztec, Indian, and Chinese. It is fascinating for a creativity researcher to consider how these ages of invention and discovery come about, what favours their emergence, how they maintain themselves through decades or even centuries, and, ultimately, what brings them to an end. Studies in this area have been done in psychology primarily by Dean Keith Simonton, whose historiometric work focused on different Golden Ages, including the Islamic one (Figure 5). His investigations, together with other types of evidence, point to the importance of great creators as role models and their effect not only on the immediately succeeding generation, but on many more afterwards.

What we should perhaps pay more attention to in the study of Golden Ages is the role played by the accumulation of creative artefacts and their distribution and availability to a wide range of people. There are many examples of Islamic art, for instance, that came to adorn interiors and public spaces, vividly illustrating the

5. Example of Islamic art, arabesque decoration at the Alhambra in Spain.

progress made not only in construction and ornamentation, but also in mathematics and, more generally, capturing a certain aesthetic and view of the world. Creative outcomes are not only the end point of the creative processes but also, in a circular manner, its beginning. They are not passive elements in the story of culture and civilization. On the contrary, people can dialogue with other creators through their productions, even when these initial creators are long gone. Moreover, artefacts themselves can reveal new features in time and be put to new uses. Such creator—audiences—object dialogues are thus emergent in nature and persistent over time. This is how, in fact, Golden Ages sometimes know a Renaissance a few centuries later.

Before unpacking further the value and role of creative outcomes for personal and societal creativity, I would like to raise a final point. A focus on creative products can add a lot to our understanding of creativity, as argued above, and it should come to complement our attention to the creator and the creative process. But focusing *only* on products is misleading. It can give the impression that all creativity is for the generation of new and valuable outcomes. In many ways, creativity has become such a popular topic nowadays because of the key role of creative production in capitalist and consumerist societies. Creativity produces economic value, even when this comes, unfortunately, at the price of inequality and environmental destruction.

But creative outcomes are also much more than this (see also Chapter 6). It is intrinsically fulfilling to work with materials and make something with one's own hands. There is often joy in creating that exceeds any financial benefits. And this is because creative outcomes contribute to our development on a personal level, not only to the development of society. Forgetting this important aspect would leave us with only a partial view of why and what we create. In the end, Golden Ages didn't just offer people an opportunity to have more creative things around them, but to better themselves.

Ideas, objects, and more

One of the prototypical outcomes of creativity is the creative idea. Having a new and original idea is so closely associated with creating that the symbol of a lit lightbulb became emblematic for creativity as a whole. The lit lightbulb stands, in this case, for insight, which is seen as an essential part of the creative process.

And yet there is much more to creativity than ideas. Thoughts need to be communicated and tried out, imaginatively or in practice, in order to prove their value and appropriateness (an important characteristic of creative outcomes besides novelty and originality). Some might argue that any creative process that was materialized into an object started from a creative idea, but this is not always the case. In fact, we often refine, update, and sometimes completely change our ideas as we engage in the material processes of making something. Creative ideas and creative objects are thus connected through bi-directional links rather than linear causality, as two sides of the same phenomenon.

In recognition of the fact that the outcomes of creativity are not only cognitive and/or material, but also cultural, I refer to all of them here as 'artefacts'. Artefacts, as products of culture, are a label we usually reserve for things valued by society, for example inventions, art installations, or designer objects. They typically reside in galleries, museums, or science labs. But we would do well, when it comes to creativity, to broaden this conception.

First of all, all products of creativity are, at the same time, cultural outcomes. This is because creators necessarily use cultural resources, from language and physical tools to sophisticated technologies, to bring them into being. Second, creative products contribute back to the range of cultural resources that are available for the creator or other people to continue their work, either by being a source of inspiration or a new tool to be put to use. This broad understanding applies from ephemeral productions such as children's drawings to Picasso's *Guernica*, from a new way to solve a maths problem in class to a breakthrough worthy of the Fields Medal. All of these are artefacts that have been created within and contribute to the culture of the home, the school, or society at large.

A key concern for creativity researchers is how to measure creative outcomes and, therefore, differentiate between those that demonstrate 'more' versus 'less' creativity. Given that, at first, creative ideas were extensively studied in empirical research, we have today quite a good grasp of how to evaluate them. Typically, creative ideas are elicited through divergent thinking tasks such as the Unusual Uses Test asking respondents to come up with as many uses as they can think of for common objects (e.g. a brick, a paperclip, a cardboard box, a pair of scissors, and so on). The list of ideas produced is analysed using four criteria: fluency or total number of ideas, flexibility or number of categories of ideas, originality or rarity of the idea, and elaboration or how well an idea is explained.

To take an example, if someone offers four uses for a brick—to build a house, to build a wall, to cook on, and to wear around one's neck as a conversation starter at a party—the fluency score is four. The flexibility score, however, is three, as building a house or a wall capture the same category of uses. To measure originality, we would need to compare these four answers with the answers of a large sample. We can assume that the building examples are low on originality (i.e. they are not rare in a larger sample of answers, being among the first most people think about for a brick), the cooking answer is probably moderately original (i.e. it might be found once or twice, especially in a large enough sample), while the ornament answer is likely to be highly original. For degree of elaboration, we notice that few details are offered for the first three items and more for the fourth.

Is this a valid way to estimate creativity? If we follow the definition of this phenomenon, we can see that novelty and originality are covered well by this measurement, but not value or appropriateness. We don't have a score, for instance, of how suitable these proposed uses would be in practice. If we did, building would score very highly but wearing a brick around one's neck would perform poorly. And here we come across a particular paradox of creative ideas. The different criteria for creativity might, in fact, be negatively related to each other. In this case, the most original answer is the least useful.

This reflects the difference between evaluating hypothetical creativity and appreciating it in real life situations. In practice, creative ideas need to strike a good balance between the conventional and the unconventional. Last but not least, ideas also depend on culture. Bricks have not been developed and used for building in all parts of the world; there are places where wood, clay, or reeds are much more common materials. Equally, cooking on bricks comes to mind more easily to those who are familiar with brick ovens. Once more, culture and context will greatly impact both creativity and its assessment.

The same observations apply when it comes to evaluating creative objects such as essays, drawings, or scientific discoveries. A person's creative output can be assessed based on number of products (fluency), their diversity (flexibility), their rarity (originality), and their level of detail (elaboration). In addition, the issue of appropriateness comes more clearly to the fore as objects are usually meant to express a feeling, solve a problem, expand our thinking, or increase our range of possibilities. Those artefacts that don't achieve any of the above are not likely to be considered creative.

Cultural context will also determine, to a great extent, how creativity is received by other people. Some cultures, particularly in the West, appreciate novelty and originality above all else and, therefore, are prone to appreciate breakthrough, radical innovation. Other cultures, especially Eastern and from the Global South, tend to value tradition more and to enjoy outcomes that continue and add to rather than disrupt what already exists.

Finally, we spoke above about ideas and material products as creative artefacts, but processes or performances (e.g. music, dance, theatre) also qualify. New criteria should probably be added for their appreciation, especially related to how easily they come together and enrich our experience. And we can also think beyond products and processes we intentionally produce as individuals. For instance, values and norms, collectively constructed, come out of rather creative negotiations between and within groups. Or one's identity and life trajectory can be thought of as a creative outcome given that they are certainly unique and (in most cases) adapted and valuable. All of these emerge, once again, out of a complex and essentially creative dialogue between self, others, and culture.

Big, little, and everything in between

Until now, we have discussed kinds of creative artefacts but didn't refer much to their creativity level. Some children's drawings might be more creative (i.e. original and valuable) than others, but they most probably won't leave as much of a mark on society as works by Salvador Dali or Frida Kahlo. This is not because the latter necessarily have 'more' creativity; indeed, if, as a society, we were to appreciate children's drawings and productions more, some might have a chance to be considered ground-breaking. It is their level of impact that differentiates these artefacts. A drawing is not usually kept for long and, even if it plays a crucial part in the child's development, it doesn't have the cultural impact of an artistic masterpiece. Another difference is the context in which these artefacts are produced (personal and familial versus professional) as well as their degree of complexity (children's drawings are typically less elaborate and don't benefit from the same level of expertise).

These observations led creativity researchers to distinguish, early on, between 'little' and 'Big' forms of creativity. Little c creativity includes all those minor, everyday products that typically don't leave a mark on culture but still matter enormously for the development and psychological health and well-being of the person. Big C creativity, on the contrary, is highly visible, revolutionary in nature, and has long-lasting effects. The former includes drawing, playing, storytelling, gardening, solving daily problems, and so on. The latter is usually separated into domains such as art, design, music, and science. Interestingly, many human activities demonstrate that little and Big C are more of a continuum. For instance, cooking can be done creatively at home, when preparing an improvised meal for the family. Award-winning chefs, however, take this activity to a new level as some of their creative artefacts get to redefine cuisine nationally or even internationally.

Examining further the idea that creative outcomes can be placed on a continuum, Kaufman and Beghetto proposed the four C model of creativity. This framework distinguishes between mini, little, Pro, and Big C. Mini c is reflected by creative ideation and creative forms of learning. This is typically the act of insight that contributes to a new understanding of things without necessarily being expressed in behaviour or available for others to evaluate. In fact, when things are being produced based on these insights, however small or ordinary they might be, we are already talking about little c. These materialized artefacts can be observed and appreciated by other people but typically don't reach beyond the creator's close relations. Pro c is creativity expressed at a professional level. It is the trained artist who is no longer a child or student, but is not at the level of Dali or Kahlo. The latter represent Big C creations, distinguished by their societal fame and impact.

Kaufman and Beghetto saw these four categories as continuous to each other rather than strictly separated. Developmentally, for instance, we start from mini and little c productions before we choose what to develop at a Pro c level. It is often, even if not always, the case that Big C creation will come out of at least a decade of Pro c activity.

An interesting addition to this model would be to consider also from whose perspective something is judged as mini, little, Pro, or Big C. And how the creator appreciates his or her own productions. There might be some thought-provoking examples here of clashes of perception between creator and audiences or between different audiences. Something that Picasso, for example, sketched one day in his youth and considered at best little c, showing it to hardly anyone, might be discovered later and gain Big C recognition at an auction or in a museum exhibition. Equally, Pro and Big C creations for audiences who lived centuries ago might be completely forgotten or become a small footnote in current history books. Time and context, once more, come to shape our view of creative outcomes.

Another important distinction that resembles the little–Big dichotomy but is not quite the same, is that between personal and historical creativity. Boden talked about P-creativity or personal creativity as producing something new from the perspective of the person, but not of society. Historical or H-creativity, on the other hand, involves novelty at a historical scale, for virtually everybody. A good example of the former is the discovery, on one's own, of the Pythagorean Theorem. This shows exceptional talent for any maths student, but it doesn't add to our general knowledge of geometry.

The distinction here is not based on the 'size' of the creative contribution, but concerns the perspectives of creator and of society. Of course, it is hard to think of society and culture as homogeneous and unitary. What passes as historical creativity for one culture might be well known in another. And, conversely, personal forms of creativity that are ignored at a certain moment in time can be re-evaluated at another and become historical.

This leads us to the question concerning the exact sub-types of Pro, Big, and historical creativity. An interesting proposition in this regard has been put forward by Sternberg and collaborators as the Propulsion Model. In their view, creative contributions can preserve current paradigms and leave the field where it is (e.g. replication and redefinition), preserve current paradigms but move the field in the direction it was already going in (e.g. forward incrementation and advance forward incrementation), reject current paradigms and try to move the field in a new direction from a pre-existing starting point (e.g. redirection and reconstruction), reject current paradigms and restart the field from a new place, helping it go in a new direction (e.g. re-initiation), or, finally, bring together elements or directions that were seen as different or even opposed (e.g. integration). It would be interesting to reflect on how these general categories might apply to little c or personal creativity as well as less conventional creative artefacts (like identity and the creativity of the life course).

In the end, it is useful to reflect on why some creative artefacts win over others, why some are treated as highly valuable outcomes while others remain invisible or are labelled as unimportant. James C. Kaufman and I considered this question in a recent paper dedicated to the CASE model (capital, awareness, spark, exceptionality). In it, we argue that most mundane artefacts are denied the label of 'creativity' because of one or more of the following factors: (a) lack of social and cultural capital on the part of the creator or, in other words, not having the 'right' education and connections to be recognized as a creator; (b) lack of awareness that one's activity is creative or at least potentially creative; (c) missing 'spark', by which we mean that the creator is not the one who had the initial creative idea but his or her work continues a path set by others; and (d) lack of exceptionality or the property of creative artefacts of standing out from other, similar productions.

Benevolent, malevolent, or both?

In the discussion here we have mostly focused on examples that demonstrate the positive impact creative outcomes have on the person and/or society. But it is undoubtedly the case that some creative artefacts have negative consequences. Indeed, if we consider the definition of creativity as leading to new, original, and valuable products we realize that people can harm others in highly original ways that they themselves, at least, can consider valuable or effective. Should we, however, call these creative? Or perhaps we need to keep associating creativity with the good side of human nature and invent a new term altogether for malicious actions and outcomes?

There are many reasons why we must reflect on *both* the positive and negative sides of creativity. First of all, we would be lacking conceptual tools to unpack malicious creative acts if we refused to consider them as creative. Second, and most important, we should avoid developing a romanticized view of creativity, creative artefacts, and people. Yes, it is the case that creativity, as we shall see in Chapter 6, is meant to open us towards the world and the worlds of other people. But this doesn't mean that some of us don't use such openness in unethical and selfish ways. Even at a personal level, creative activity and its outcomes can have both positive and negative consequences. For example, if someone is very good at solving problems in a quick, improvised manner, he or she might lose the habit of checking instructions or following rules, even when the latter are crucial for one's safety.

Any discussion of creative artefacts and morality needs to distinguish between intentions and results. If someone wants to create a thing that improves the lives of others, but his or her creation gets to be used (also) for negative ends, is the creator to blame? Should we accuse the creator of dynamite, Alfred Nobel, for it harming people in military conflicts? Or Oppenheimer for the destruction caused by the atomic bomb?

These are difficult questions to answer, given that we might not always know exactly the intentions of creative people or understand fully their context. However, it is widely accepted today that 'malevolent creativity' involves the emergence of creative outcomes that are intended to cause harm. And there are many illustrations of new and surprising creative acts that are fundamentally destructive in nature, for instance unconventional terrorist attacks.

Things become more complex when we consider that harming others can sometimes seem justifiable, for example in war situations. Using new, original, and highly effective ways to destroy one's enemies can turn someone into a hero or a villain, a martyr or an outcast. And this might bring about one and the same person being viewed by different groups as benevolent or malevolent, respectively. Of course, one can argue that we have international organizations and conventions that are meant to assess the morality of war actions, for instance. But these organizations and their decisions often remain contested.

To complicate things further, people do things for different reasons, some altruistic, some egotistic, some reflecting both at once. This resembles to some extent the discussion about intrinsic and extrinsic motivation from Chapter 2. Instead of a black and white statement about malevolent and benevolent creativity, we are thus left with some clear examples of each and a considerable amount of grey zone instances and artefacts.

Asking creators directly what their intentions are doesn't help much either, as people naturally tend to believe they are doing the right thing or convince themselves they are. How else can we explain the environmental destruction and impoverishment of local communities by people who act in the name of capitalism, productivity, and neoliberalism?

Many of them trust, after all, that the end goals of producing more goods and money justify the costs. This might be written off as an example of unintended consequences but, in fact, it is one of bad faith and self-serving biases. Big corporations are often very creative today in the way they acquire and exploit natural resources around the globe, something Sierra and Fallon talked about as examples of 'exploitative creativity'. The creative outcomes, in this case, are considerable wealth for a few and poverty, displacement, even genocide for others, not to mention the collective price of climate change.

To end on a more positive note, there are also many examples of how new and positive consequences can come out of a creative product in an unexpected manner. Referred to as exaptation, the process of discovering new functions for existing artefacts is richly illustrated in the fields of medicine and technology. This is how, for instance, a tuberculosis treatment ended up leading to the development of antidepressants. Or how a weak glue that didn't seem to serve any purpose for a decade led to the invention of Post-it notes. Of course, in most of these cases it is not the original creator who gets to envision new functions and possibilities. But such illustrations of 'solutions waiting for a problem' make us aware of what Corazza called the inconclusiveness of creative artefacts. We can never foresee all the possible uses, positive and negative, of creative products at the moment of their making.

This is an important last observation when it comes to the distinction between product and process in creativity. It is commonly assumed that a creative product is the end point of the creative process but, as I've briefly shown above, products do initiate new creative processes, including in other people. They are two facets of the same coin. The 'what' and the 'how' of creativity are connected through the passing of time. In time, creative artefacts get to be used, forgotten, rediscovered, and sometimes completely reinvented. The processes through which these transformations take place are the focus of Chapter 4.

Chapter 4
The how of creativity

Arguably one of the most fascinating yet difficult questions to answer when it comes to creativity concerns the nature of the creative process. How exactly creativity happens has been a topic of reflection for centuries, if not millennia, well before we had a word for this phenomenon or studied it with the means of science. And yet, many centuries later, we are still missing a comprehensive view of creative processes or a clear understanding of their complexity.

This is unsurprising in many ways. If creativity concerns the emergence of the unexpected, to some extent, then it is pointless to propose predictive or deterministic models for it. If we knew exactly how creativity works and followed its 'formula', it wouldn't be creativity any more. At the same time, we have accumulated considerable knowledge, especially over the past seventy years, into the psychological traits, skills, and mechanisms that contribute to creative production. We have a longer way to go when it comes to integrating emotions, the body, material objects, other people, institutions, and culture into the story of creativity.

In this chapter, we will take a closer look at creative processes. I am not using the singular—process—deliberately as there are many ways to be creative, at once personal and contextual. Moreover, each one of these ways or processes is multidimensional. While we tend to think that creativity starts 'in the head', in the form of ideas that get to be realized (or not) afterwards, the cognitive dimension is only one among many. We wouldn't be able to have creative ideas in the first place, if we didn't have a brain to support ideation and a body that allows movement and is receptive to the environment. As such, there is also a neurological and embodied aspect to creative cognition.

Beyond cognition itself, creativity is driven by different motives and coloured by a variety of emotions. We don't simply think when creating, but also feel and experience special states of consciousness such as wonder, awe, and flow. Other people matter as well. Not only is it the case that we create with and for others, but social interactions offer us the 'material' to think about, feel into, and act upon. Last but not least, creating means making, and no form of making is possible outside of a physical universe 'populated' by objects with their different properties and affordances.

These psychological (cognitive, emotional, and motivational), social, and material dimensions of the creative process are connected to each other within what I call creative action. Action is a notion that integrates psychological and behavioural manifestations into a unit—doing—that is at once individual and cultural. Indeed, our actions are different from biological reflexes and automatic responses. They reflect the cultural nature of our existence by making use of the symbols, signs, and the many tools and resources available within society.

To take a basic example, walking is a common behaviour involving the movement of our legs and body that takes us from point A to point B. But, as an action, it implies preparing to walk somewhere by wearing appropriate shoes, regulating the speed and rhythm of our walk to what is appropriate in a given circumstance, being able to think about whether we actually want to walk or take the bus, and, for some people, checking at the end of the day how much they walked on their mobile app and making plans for the week.

How does all of this apply to creativity? If creative processes were merely biological, they would involve little intentionality, be void of meaning, and ignore social context. As an action, however, creativity becomes goal oriented, meaningful, and shaped by cultural norms and values. For some, the latter might sound curious as creating is thought of in terms of breaking with the existing culture in order to generate the new. Conformity to society and culture seems antithetical to creativity itself. A closer examination proves the contrary. No acts of creation can exist independent of culture, even if many creators react to what is considered 'mainstream' culture. Highly creative people aim to overcome social conventions and antiquated norms and values, but they necessarily do so by using other conventions and adhering to the norms and values of other, marginal groups in society.

The example of Impressionist painters in the late 19th century is useful here. Claude Monet and Pierre-Auguste Renoir did react to the artistic establishment—the *Académie* and its *Salon de Paris*—but did so while collaborating with fellow painters and upholding newly formed conventions and even institutions (e.g. the *Salon des Refusés*). Through them, a fringe culture became mainstream and a new avant-garde was called for in the 20th century.

What we understand better about the 'how' of creativity when considering it in terms of action is precisely how individual acts make use of, react to, and ultimately contribute to a certain history and culture. Without this cultural-historical perspective, we would be left to analyse creative processes as purely individual (re)constructions of ideas without any specific origins, expression, and consequences. The fact that to create means to act in and on the world in new and meaningful ways invites us to consider the role of this 'world' in enabling, guiding, and, at times, constraining our possibilities for creative action.

The best illustrations of the role of culture in creativity come from examining everyday actions and interactions. For instance, craft activities offer us a great example of how creative ideas, the body, material objects, and cultural traditions come together in producing new artefacts of societal significance. In previous research, I examined Easter egg decoration practices as a creative activity that reveals the complex ecosystem mentioned here.

Egg decoration requires the constant recombination of cultural patterns and motifs, highly developed embodied skills, the support of specialized material tools, and knowledge of their affordances (see Figure 6). Unlike what most would assume, traditional decoration doesn't involve applying pigments on the egg with a brush but drawing the motifs with melted wax and immersing the

6. Easter egg decorated by Valerica Jusca in the village of Ciocanesti, northern Romania.

egg periodically in colour (from lighter to darker hues). The principle is that those parts covered by wax will keep the colour under them. As such, working on the egg requires special cognitive abilities and a lot of practice as it essentially means drawing on a negative image. It is only at the end, cleaning off the wax, that the actual pattern is revealed.

Far from crafts involving repetitive, automatic, and basically uncreative actions, a closer examination of egg decoration shows that there are no identical Easter eggs and that this practice involves mastery, tradition, and culture as preconditions for creativity.

This study also questions other assumptions about the creative process, such as the fact that it takes place in distinct, successive phases. Graham Wallas, the author of the influential *Art of Thought*, famously proposed almost a century ago the four stages of preparation, incubation, illumination, and verification as essential for creativity. The first involves acquiring all the resources necessary to create. The second presupposes a moment of letting go of creative work and focusing on something else. This unconscious incubation leads to the creative idea—the moment of insight or illumination. Finally, it takes some checking of whether the idea is applicable or useful. If this is not the case, the cycle can start from the beginning.

While there is something reassuring in identifying the main phases of a creative activity and labelling them, we can also see how the four stages above don't apply in each and every case. If we return to the example of egg decoration, preparation doesn't involve only setting up a workspace but includes the period, sometimes years, of practising decoration. Incubation and illumination might not be distinct stages at all but represent micro-moments in a continuous work process. Most creative ideas come from doing and the many happy accidents and discoveries occasioned by what has been done before on the egg. Verification remains important—the moment when the wax is removed from the egg and the quality of the final product is checked. But here, again, new things tend to be learned during verification, which, in many ways, is thus part of the preparation for future creativity.

It is because of this back and forth, non-linear character of creative action that stage models such as that proposed by Wallas have been complemented, if not altogether replaced, by a focus on ongoing processes. Unfortunately, the latter are considered, at least in psychology, primarily in cognitive terms. What I will do in this chapter is unpack different types of processes involved in creative action—psychological, social, and material—processes that, even if treated below in separate sections, are fundamentally intertwined.

Psychological processes of creativity

For most people the 'origin' of creativity, as well as the 'place' where it unfolds, is the brain or the mind of the creator. As such, over a few centuries, we developed a highly psychological vocabulary for the creative process. The focus of this vocabulary is on cognition or thinking processes. This is how, for instance, we talk today about creativity as divergent, combinatorial, or lateral thinking and associate it with insight or creative ideation. While such descriptions are by and large reductionist, there is certainly a close connection between cognitive and creative processes. If creativity uses previous knowledge in ways that result in new knowledge, then thinking or cognition certainly plays an important part in it.

One of the oldest ways of conceiving the creative process is based on the notion of association of ideas. According to this view, to create means to put together two or more disparate ideas and combine them. Imagining a unicorn means, basically, adding a horn to a regular horse. Or making a purse in the shape of a banana brings together the idea of a container with that of fruit.

The more different the domain of each idea, the more surprising the creative outcome. For example, art and trash are things typically kept separate not only by their appearance but also by their assumed value. But artists like Sara Goldschmied and Eleonora Chiari created an installation called 'Where are we going dancing tonight?' depicting the mess and leftovers from a party. Unsurprisingly, however, too much creativity can backfire. The exhibition referred to here made the news when museum cleaners binned it by mistake, confusing it with actual trash. One's creative associations can certainly trigger different associations in the minds of others.

Combinatorial models of the creative process are fundamentally based on the simple notion that ideas can be combined with each other, resulting in novel associations. This raises the question of whether an idea can indeed be combined with any other. Isn't it more likely that we would associate ideas that more naturally come together in conventional ways?

Dean Keith Simonton disagrees with this. In his Blind Variation Selective Retention (BVSR) model, inspired by evolutionary perspectives, he postulates that in fact the combinatorial phase is 'blind' or random. There is little intentionality in how ideas collide and mix in our thinking, producing often truly unexpected outcomes. What 'tames' the originality of this process, however, is the stage of selective retention when, as the name suggests, only those combinations that show promise (either in terms of being more meaningful or easier to apply in practice) are actually kept. We thus constantly create new ideas in our mind, but mostly remember those with some kind of value for us. How 'blind' this combinatorial process is remains contested, though, especially when we take into account the fact that cultural norms tend to give our ideation a specific pattern and kind of predictability.

Another version of a cognitive model of creativity is represented by the Geneplore model by Roland Finke, Thomas Ward, and

Steven Smith. The name of this model is, itself, based on word combination—generate and explore. These are, according to the three authors, the two interdependent phases of the creative process in which we constantly come up with ideas and quickly explore them, leading to new ideas and new exploration. Ideas are called in this model 'preinventive structures' in order to designate the fact that, until they are properly explored and tested, they carry creative potential but are not yet creative.

The two phases of generation and exploration are integrated, that is, one constantly feeds the other leading to focusing or expanding the initial concept. Despite the fact that product constraints are recognized as important—in the sense that we take into account the limits of what we can do or hope to achieve—this framework remains excessively cognitive and largely oblivious to the materiality of the creative process. Preinventive structures are never sketches made on paper or prototypes in clay, but mental representations. The process is once more placed in the head instead of the hands and the world (as well).

The same critique applies to the notions of divergent and convergent thinking. As I mentioned in Chapter 3, divergent thinking involves coming up with multiple solutions or answers for an open-ended task. Convergent thinking, on the contrary, results in a single, correct answer. While the former is certainly associated with creativity, there is growing evidence that convergence has its own part to play in the creative process. After all, the BVSR and Geneplore models both postulate the dynamic between a phase of open exploration (blind variation or generation, respectively) and a phase that is somewhat narrow or focused (selective retention or exploration, respectively). What convergent thinking contributes to the creative process is probably best reflected in the evaluation of creative ideas. While we can ideate considerably about a problem—the main feature of brainstorming—we also need, by the end, to choose the best solution available.

There is yet another cognitive dimension to creativity left unexplored until now, and that is insight. Insight corresponds to the illumination or 'aha' moment referred to in Wallas's four-stage model. It is the instantaneous grasp of a solution that doesn't go through divergent routes of exploration. Or, at least, it doesn't seem like it does. While insights famously 'come out of nowhere', research shows that, in fact, we often have partial or mini moments of insight before coming up with the unexpected solution we were looking for. We are just bad at remembering these steps as we focus on the final, surprising outcome. Whereas creative insight cannot be trained as easily as divergent thinking, there are ways in which, by solving insight problems and opening our mind to unexpected solutions, we can invite 'eureka' moments into our life and work. Most of them need to be further explored and selectively retained, as mentioned above, given that not all insights—as delightful and surprising as they might be—are equally useful.

Finally, we should ask ourselves if the psychological processes of creating are all cognitive or thought based. Certainly not. Our ideas, in fact, are coloured by emotion and related to what excites or worries us at a given moment (see Chapter 2). Besides, if the underlying dynamic of creativity is combinatorial, then idea associations don't always follow reason but emotion. Dictionary relations between concepts, specifying what connects to what in which way, are never used as such in creative work. If this were the case, then we could predetermine the emergence of a certain association given what we know about the semantic relation between two concepts. But this relation in our mind is highly idiosyncratic and based on how we feel about ideas and the things they designate. For example, a child who loves eating ice-cream while visiting the local zoo might associate it with seeing meerkats and, one day, imagine what meerkat-shaped ice-cream could look like. Needless to say, this is a rare thought in children or adults for whom the two exist as distant semantic categories.

Social processes of creativity

All the processes mentioned above are highly individual in nature. Even when our thoughts and emotions are conceived as coming out of interactions with the environment, these interactions are placed in the background rather than at the centre of creativity. One particular process that is crucially important for creative expression, though, is represented by exchanging ideas with other people. It is not only the case that we often create in collaboration with others, for instance when we work in teams, but we need their knowledge and skills most of the time to turn initial ideas into concrete outcomes. In the end, creative achievement comes out of division of labour within society in which different groups of people contribute to different parts of a broader, collective creative process.

Moreover, the social dimension of creativity is at play even when creating in solitude. This might be a harder notion to grasp but think, for example, about how the views of other people influence us beyond our immediate encounters with them. We all 'carry' with us the perspectives of family, friends, mentors, and even critics and competitors. How these come to shape creative work, done alone or with others, is of concern for us in this section.

Let's first have a closer look at how people create together. Groupwork should normally benefit creative production as different people will most certainly have different types of knowledge, skills, and perspectives on a given problem or situation. In this regard, one would expect that the more heterogeneous the group, the higher the likelihood of reaching a creative outcome. And yet, this is not guaranteed. As we all know from our own experiences of groupwork, sometimes things go smoothly and sometimes there is tension, even conflict between group members.

In other words, beside the psychological dynamic of each person, we need to take into account the social dimension of the relations between them. When harmonious, these relations can generate a feeling of flow conducive for creativity. But they might also lead to groupthink or the tendency to agree with each other and enforce a common, group identity. Tension can be positive or negative. Disagreement is actually one of the main engines of creativity given that it forces group members to consider the perspectives of others and see their own perspective through their eyes. And yet, when it turns into conflict, this openness towards the other is compromised.

Alex Osborn created brainstorming in the 1950s based on the assumption that receiving criticism from others, even when it is well intentioned, is counterproductive. It makes people get into an evaluative mode rather than a generative one. Or, according to the BVSR model, it reduces the chances of highly original, blind variations of ideas by focusing us too much on selective retention. In order to remove the pressure of evaluation, Osborn imposed a 'no criticisms' rule in brainstorming based on the assumption that 'quantity will lead to quality'. In essence, the more ideas people produce together, the higher the chances that at least some of them will be valuable (when evaluated at a later stage).

Brainstorming is meant to inspire everyone through the opportunity to listen to the ideas of others. But, as empirical research soon came to show, there are also many downsides to this practice. First of all, by having to listen to others, one might lose focus and forget his or her own ideas. Or, worse yet, he or she might not find any space to express them. This phenomenon is called in the literature 'production blocking'. And there are other dangers as well. For example, we might be prompted to follow the same line of thinking set by the others. Conforming, even involuntarily, to the emergent group consensus takes us into dangerous groupthink territory. What is there to do?

While experimental research demonstrated that individuals working alone tend to produce more and better ideas than groups, this is no reason to dismiss groupwork or even brainstorming. In fact, the research referred to above typically uses artificial settings and tasks (e.g. asking people how many things they can do with a brick, a generic divergent thinking task that doesn't take into account the background and motivation of the participants) and asks strangers to collaborate for a mere ten to fifteen minutes. Real life contexts are different from this. At the workplace, for instance, we usually know who we are collaborating with and have a history of working together. The tasks we work on are also more meaningful and usually correspond to our expertise and interests. In other words, finding creative solutions matters much more and, together with a better understanding of collaborators, can lead to improved performance, including during brainstorming sessions.

One remaining question is what exactly are the social processes that contribute to creativity. The dynamic between members of a group can shape the way ideas are raised, accepted, or rejected, but does it contribute to the ideas themselves? In order to understand this, we need to consider what exactly people exchange during their interaction. More than concrete ideas, they share their perspective or way of approaching the problem at hand. From the perspective of a parent, for instance, the perfect toy would be safe to use and make little noise. From that of a child, it would be colourful and loud. From a designer's point of view, the quality of the materials and sustainability would matter most. Finally, a doctor would consider the chemicals involved in producing a toy for young children. It is from expressing and exchanging these perspectives—including being able to take the perspective of others—that a creative outcome can be reached, through dialogue.

Perspective-taking and dialogue thus emerge as key social processes involved in creative expression. They come to complement the discussion about combination and divergence, insight and evaluation of ideas from the previous section. Indeed, if we replace 'ideas' with 'perspectives' and consider the fact that all of them have a social origin and impact, we get to understand how, even when working alone, we are still dialoguing with the internalized views of others. As I write these pages of what, with any luck, is at least a partially creative introduction to creativity, I recurrently think of you, my reader, and try to anticipate what might be important for you or sound confusing. I manage to do this because I am a reader myself, of my own work and the work of others. I thus build on my social experience to take different perspectives (successfully, hopefully) and to create a new text with their help.

Material processes of creativity

There is yet another dimension to creating that is even less incorporated, at least in psychology, than the social one—materiality. This is rather surprising given that, as I mentioned in Chapters 1 and 3, the very definition of creativity is product based. We identify creative processes by considering their outcomes in terms of novelty, originality, and value. These outcomes can be an idea but very often they are material objects. Either way, there is a degree of materialization of creative ideas either in language or through acts of making. Ultimately, making stands as one of the paradigmatic ways of being creative by producing something with one's hands. What is specific for such material processes?

One aspect that stands out is tinkering. At all ages, creative people tend to explore their environment and manipulate the objects within it in ways that lead to new insights and forms of doing. Experimentation or trial and error is a fundamental process through which creativity proceeds within embodied action. This type of exploration might be driven by certain goals or completely open to what will happen next. Inviting (happy) accidents and the unexpected helps us discover new sides of or uses for the objects surrounding us. As such, serendipitous moments are part and parcel of the material processes of creating either alone or with others. New perspectives can be invited by interacting with other people as well as with material objects. And these perspectives change our position towards the task or problem at hand, helping us see it in a new light.

But what exactly are we discovering when we manipulate objects? One important feature when it comes to creativity is captured by the notion of affordance. A term coined initially by J. J. Gibson, affordances are basically what the objects surrounding us allow us to do with them (what they afford our action).

For example, cups have the affordance of drinking from them, pencils that of writing, and flashlights afford light. These are not generic and universal properties of objects, however. If the cup is broken, it doesn't afford holding liquid any more; if the pencil is not sharpened, it can't really leave marks on paper; and if the flashlight is out of battery, it won't produce any light. And then there is also the contribution of the person using them. These objects have the affordances just mentioned above for a human being—an animal without hands or opposable thumbs wouldn't normally be able to hold a pencil, let alone write with it. And human babies don't notice this affordance either. Or, if an adult is in a completely dark room, and doesn't see the flashlight sitting on the table, he or she won't enact the affordance of creating light. One can ultimately identify here the contribution of culture. If we take a person who doesn't live in a culture that produces flashlights, he or she wouldn't be able to enact its affordance unless discovered by accident, through tinkering.

In summary, affordances are not 'located' within physical objects—they depend on the relationship between object properties and the abilities of the person, both in view of a broader culture. Affordances aren't thus 'natural' categories only, in the sense that, as human beings, we get to almost immediately perceive some of them (e.g. we typically know when something in

63

front of us is solid or liquid and thus if we can step on it or not), but, most of the time, the perception and use of affordances depends on learning. We need to have learnt what different objects are for in order to enact their affordances. Gibson noted in this regard that people who don't know about mailboxes and the post won't be able to use them to send a letter (or write one).

What does all this have to do with creativity? Well, in the examples above I specified one affordance for each object, one that is central for it. Cups are for drinking, but they can also be put to many other uses. A big cup can become a paper holder on a windy day, it can hold a door open or become a container for small objects, including jewellery. The fact that we don't usually use cups like this doesn't mean we couldn't, especially when the right situation arises. And this is what creativity is mostly about. It designates the process by which we bypass the canonical or dominant affordance of an object in order to discover and make use of alternative, unexpected affordances. An artist, for example, when inspired by the found object perspective in art, might sign a common cup or a flashlight and call it an artwork.

The material processes of creativity invite us thus to discover new affordances and make use of them. But they cannot be separated from the psychological and social dimension of creating. The meaning we typically give to things and the cultural norms involved in their use both matter for embodied ideation and exploration.

In the end, what we can conclude about the 'how' of creativity is that it equally depends on psychological, social, and material factors and, most of all, on their interdependence. The combinatorial dynamic of creativity, at a psychological level, requires social interaction in order to gain access to perspectives and ideas that will be placed in dialogue with each other. These new perspectives are inspired by other people, but they can also derive from the accidental discovery of affordances during a playful manipulation of objects.

Creative action also depends on what has been done before. For instance, things that initially required a lot of attention and practice to get right become habitual over time. This doesn't mean that they lose their creative quality altogether. Highly skilled musicians, for instance, have practised their actions enough times that they become part of a routine. This routine is never fully automatic, however, and musicians deal with small problems and obstacles as they come. This is, after all, what makes them masterful practitioners. Easter egg decorators, referred to at the start, are another good example of this category.

This basic creative quality of everyday, rehearsed actions I have called in the past 'habitual creativity'. It is distinct from instances in which we don't have a practised solution, cases that require improvisation. Improvisational creativity is marked by the fact that our action is stopped by a challenge it needs to overcome. If and when we make the conscious decision to overcome this challenge creatively, we enter the realm of innovative creativity. Such a choice will depend, however, on the time and energy we have at our disposal, as well as on the context, which should welcome innovation and make it safe or OK to take risks. This context, the when and where of creativity, is what concerns us next.

Chapter 5
The when and where of creativity

We have focused so far on the creative person, product, and process, every time emphasizing how context—material, social, and cultural—matters for each of them. We concluded, for example, that any study of the creator shouldn't focus exclusively on personal attributes but consider how these attributes developed within a specific environment. Understanding creative outcomes also requires a contextual approach. If nothing else because qualities such as novelty, originality, and value are context dependent. Finally, the creative process is not only psychological, but equally social and material. This means that creativity happens 'in between' people and places rather than 'within' them.

It isn't enough though to claim that context matters, we also need to understand how. In this chapter, I will focus on the temporal (when) and socio-material (where) dimensions of context when it comes to creativity. And the main argument I want to put forward is that time, space, and other people are much more than a background or set of factors that come to influence, from the outside, the creative person, product, and process. The 'when' and 'where' of creativity are an integral part of this phenomenon, given that they offer the means for creative action, set the standards for it, and guide its course.

A simple thought experiment can demonstrate this. Imagine that creativity did, in fact, take place only inside the mind of the creator and this mind would exist outside any physical, social, or temporal context—basically outside time and space. Where would this creative mind obtain the sensorial stimuli (e.g. images, sounds, smells) that form the basis for creative ideation? Arguably, it wouldn't have anything to combine and recombine in the absence of a sensorial input coming from the body in its encounter with the environment. Moreover, there would be no other people around it to interact with. One might think that this is not necessarily a bad thing, as many creative ideas come when we are alone. But the fact that no other people exist means that language and culture don't either. The meanings we work with in the creative process, including the meaning we assign to what we create, would be gone as well. In the end, this solitary mind wouldn't be able to even know if a creative thought occurred to it, far less appreciate its value. They all depend on context.

If context is so important, this means that creative processes are contingent, to a large extent, on when and where the creator is. For instance, we express our creativity differently at home or at school compared to the workplace. More generally, the domain of activity is highly consequential. The creative actions of an artist normally differ from those of an engineer. Going further, the way we express ourselves creatively as children is different from how we act as adults and different again from creativity in old age.

These observations all sound plausible. They support a view of creativity as domain and age specific. And yet, there are also some creativity researchers who believe in domain generality. They typically point to the fact that someone who has creative skills and a creative approach to life would normally express them at home and at work, in creating a poem as well as approaching a maths problem, in childhood as well as in adulthood. In other words, there are some basic traits and processes (e.g. divergent thinking;

67

if you don't recall it, please revisit Chapter 4) that cut across contexts and domains.

Who is right? In many ways, both domain-general and domain-specific advocates have a point. It all depends on what aspects of creativity they are talking about. We can certainly list features such as openness to experience and tolerance for ambiguity that are likely to be useful for all creative actions. But there are many more aspects of it that will depend on the situation. Context, once more, is not simply the background against which creativity takes place, but an important part of it. This, finally, is the 'generalizable' truth about creating.

The Amusement Park Theory (APT) proposed by James C. Kaufman and John Baer is perhaps the best-known framework to acknowledge the largely domain-specific nature of creativity. Its name comes from the analogy between creating and visiting an amusement park.

Initially, there will always be some general requirements to enter a park, such as money for the ticket. This translates, in the case of creativity, into a certain level of intelligence, motivation, personality traits, and a favourable environment. When in possession of these minimum requirements, one has to make several choices. First, which kind of amusement park to visit. Then, what actual park from the kind chosen. And, on the day, what to do within the park itself. This is what Kaufman and Baer call the general thematic area, domains, and micro-domains of creativity, respectively. If we are to take the example of creativity in the arts, the general thematic area is art, the domain might be visual arts, and the micro-domain the paintings, videos, or installations being created. Each one of these will influence the creative process and determine its different standards for success and failure.

It's interesting to notice, when it comes to domains, that certain fields of activity are automatically considered more creative than others. When someone defines himself or herself as an artist, for instance, we are generally inclined to consider that person at least potentially creative. Faced with a mathematician, we might doubt whether this quality is required. In the end, all fields of human activity depend on creativity, even if some of them enable or constrain it more than others.

Given that, in the West at least, novelty and originality are typically valued more than usefulness, all those domains that require a break with the past and radical innovation are immediately catalogued as creative. In contrast, in many Eastern cultures, creativity is valued when it leads to incremental change and when it continues rather than breaks with tradition. The first kind of response is typical for the arts, and the second one for crafts and craftsmanship. As we saw in Chapter 4 in the case of Easter egg decoration, creative processes can be found even within traditional craft. It is cultural context that will determine, finally, how visible or appreciated this kind of creativity is.

But there is more to context than the norms, values, and institutions of a social and cultural environment. Contexts are principally made up of objects, people, and places. These range from the immediate environment of the creators, including for example the home and the workplace, to more distant environments such as the neighbourhoods or communities the creator is part of. Speaking of workspaces, it is interesting to study the ways in which creative people arrange them, the things they collect, how they organize objects, who is allowed to visit and when, etc. An artist's studio comes to mind here as a prototypical place where creativity happens.

For example, Constantin Brâncuşi, the Romanian sculptor considered by many one of the fathers of modernism, worked in a studio in Paris that has been reconstructed today across from the Pompidou Centre in Paris (Figure 7). This studio included not only tools and materials, but also finished and unfinished

7. *Mademoiselle Pogany* by Constantin Brâncuşi.

sculptures and other artefacts. The main purpose of this accumulation of things is, undeniably, to inspire the creator, even if to an outside observer most artist spaces look messy and impossible to work in.

As research shows, however, creative people are not only inspired by their own work; they also look for and keep the creations of others. This is why, when it comes to the broader environment of not only artists but also designers, scientists, and inventors, it is important to identify those material spaces in which people meet, discuss, and encounter the ideas and products of peers. Golden Ages, as noted in Chapter 3, depend on both the availability of role models and a wide range of accumulated artefacts. Beyond these predictable encounters, opportunities to immerse oneself in the life of specific communities, especially marginal ones, serve as a source of insight and creative ideas. Henri de Toulouse-Lautrec famously frequented brothels where he painted women in everyday situations. Marginal spaces foster unconventional sights and these, in turn, nurture the creativity of those already inclined to notice the unusual and make creative use of it.

Time for creativity

There is something intrinsically important about the relation between creativity and time. Not only does it take time to create, but creative action itself should always be situated within its time in order to be understood better. And there are multiple temporal dimensions to be taken into account.

The widest of them all is called phylogenesis and it refers to the development of the species. Indeed, if being creative has been a distinguishing quality for humanity since its very beginning, then we should reflect on today's creativity in view of this much longer past. This includes the discovery of fire and its uses, the domestication of animals, the birth of agriculture, the construction of houses and cities, the development of language, both spoken and written, and the emergence of art, first depicted in caves and then ornamenting most tools used by humans. Of course, these acts of creativity took hundreds of thousands of years to happen, to be exercised and perfected. They might all be things considered basic, primitive, or normal today but, without them, human civilization would not have started.

Given that biologically we are not significantly different from our direct ancestors, the first *Homo sapiens* who lived about 300,000 years ago, we might wonder why the first creations took so long to come about while currently we seem to hear about new inventions every other day. It cannot be the case that we have a bigger, more performant brain, so what makes the difference is certainly the environment. Human culture is cumulative, which means that its members can rely on the artefacts and knowledge of previous generations. The children of today don't have to reinvent the wheel, as it were, or rediscover the latest scientific theories. It is because of this rich and stimulating environment, and the progress in education theory and practice, that we create standing on the shoulders of many giants.

What a study of phylogenesis does is to situate recent artefacts against a much wider, species-specific background. But, while biological constraints and evolutionary tendencies can only go so far when it comes to understanding 'modern' creativity, another temporal line—sociogenesis—becomes crucial. Basically, sociogenesis designates the evolution of society and its documentation as human history. The birth of philosophy and religion, the development of the arts and sciences, the changes in political organization, as well as the growth, peaks, and disappearance of civilizations are all part of it. Sociogenesis, although much more 'recent' (starting with recorded history, around the 4th millennium BC), is key for understanding the shape and content of creative domains today.

For example, knowledge of the history of art is important for any contemporary artist. It is not only the case that current techniques, tools, and sources of inspiration have been shaped by diverse civilizations (e.g. Egyptian, Greek, Japanese, French), but, in order to understand why a contemporary artist would make little effort to capture reality 'as it is', we need to consider the big ruptures within this long history. If two centuries ago, before the emergence and widespread use of photography, painters were judged on their ability to depict a person or scene realistically, the 20th century witnessed new and radical ideologies in art. From the emphasis on emotion and perception characteristic of Impressionists, to the abstract, geometrical style of Cubists, the art of today would be unrecognizable to 17th-century Dutch masters. And yet, there are also solid bridges, across time, between contemporary art and, for instance, the hieroglyphs of ancient Egypt and resonances with the use of shadow and light by Rembrandt. Sociogenesis thus includes both discontinuities and continuities and provides the societal background against which each new creation is evaluated as new, important, ground-breaking, or more of the same.

Until now we have discussed mostly the creativity of adults, the ones who are generally able to leave their mark on history. What about children and old people? Another temporal dimension comes to the fore when we consider the development of the person—ontogenesis. It goes without saying that creative expression will differ in its content, processes, and consequence, across the lifespan. It is by paying attention to these differences that we get to understand something else essential about creativity.

For instance, studying how it begins in early childhood can shed a new light on its expression (or lack of) in adults. It is commonly assumed that the first manifestations of creativity emerge during moments of pretend play from one and a half to two years of age. It is when children become capable of using words and meanings to describe reality that an essential shift takes place in their relationship with it. Instead of being confined to perceiving and using things as they are, children can rename and re-signify what is in front of them and act 'as if' it was different. For instance, a small piece of wood can become a car, a banana can be a phone, and a piece of rope can play the part of a snake. Pretence doesn't mean confusing things for what they are not but developing a much more flexible relation to objects, aided by meanings and culture. And this takes us back to sociogenesis and shows how intertwined the temporalities discussed here really are.

I mentioned bananas being used as a phone but, in fact, the

old-style receptors are rapidly replaced by flat-looking mobile and smart phones. Children's creativity and play will necessarily reflect such changes.

And so will adult creativity. While we might lose some of the flexibility and playfulness of children's expression, adults are likely to take the norms, values, and constraints of their society and culture into account. The latter will lead to more appropriate and valuable outcomes, but lack some of the spontaneity and originality of children's productions. As people grow older, their creativity doesn't necessarily follow a downward trajectory. In fact, depending on the culture they live in (knowing, for instance, that collectivist cultures tend to respect their elders much more than individualistic ones) and the domain of activity (since in some domains, such as the sciences, big discoveries tend to be made later in life compared to art), old age creativity becomes a more or less distant possibility.

Last but not least when it comes to creativity and time, we have microgenesis, or the moment to moment unfolding of creative action. If we go back to the example of a painter, this concerns the gradual application of paint on the canvas. For children's play, this is reflected in the 'stages' of first selecting toys and then playing with them. A close analysis of microgenesis is what most creativity researchers attempt when they study the creative process. Where does it start? What are its different phases? How do we proceed from one to the other? Chapter 4 addressed many of these questions.

Here it is worth making one additional observation, related to the passage of time: the conditions of future action are, each moment, set by what has been done before. This is obvious in the artist's work, whenever he or she stands back to evaluate what was just painted and how to proceed. The artist will also use his or her life experience and artistic expertise to make such judgements. Equally, children's play retakes themes and scenarios played before, including those seen at home, at the kindergarten, or on television. In the end, microgenesis is framed by ontogenesis which, in turn, depends on sociogenesis and phylogenesis. All of these embedded temporal contexts are crucial for creative expression.

Spaces for creativity

The passing of time is primarily marked by changes in the spaces and objects that make up our environment. The physical environment in particular has received little attention within creativity research. This is because of the common assumption, discussed at length in this book, that creating is primarily a mental activity. And yet, as I have also argued here, creativity is not only embodied but creative processes are as much material as they are psychological. In fact, we wouldn't be able to talk about any psychological process if we lacked a brain, a body, and an environment made up of objects and their affordances.

The little work on physical environments and their impact on creativity has been done at the workplace and in relation to the discipline of ergonomics. Jan Dul and Canan Ceylan, for instance, have studied the positive relation between certain material features at work and creative expression, including the arrangement of the furniture, the presence of indoor plants, calming and inspiring colours, window views to nature, quality of light and the presence of daylight, temperature and humidity of the air, and positive sounds and odours. While more studies need to be done to identify the effect of each, it is most probably their presence together that influences the state of mind and well-being of creative people. More than this, it is their interaction with other features of work, studied as well by Dul and Ceylan, that matter most (e.g. a challenging job, good teamwork, autonomy, a coaching supervisor, time for thinking, freedom to set creative goals and incentives to achieve them).

What these call to our attention when it comes to spaces for creativity is the fact that social and material aspects are not separate from each other. Indeed, a physical work environment favourable for creativity, one in which people have enough space to move around, de-connect at times, meet others and collaborate, is usually put together by managers who care for their employees, for their creativity and their occasions to collaborate. The norms and values of companies and institutions also matter here. In the end, this is how permission to work with others and the physical affordances to do so get to be inscribed into a wider work or organizational culture. Without necessarily being made explicit, these opportunities are inscribed in how people do things and the things they do.

Of course, organizational cultures are part of wider regional, national, and global counterparts. Geert Hofstede famously studied the dimensions of work cultures with a view towards the national context. He devised different indexes, including for power distance, individualism vs collectivism, uncertainty avoidance, masculinity vs femininity, long-term vs short-term orientations. It is tempting to assume, from these, that environments that reflect a lower distance to power (so have a less hierarchical structure) or show lower uncertainty avoidance (thus accepting more easily the unexpected) are more conducive for creativity. This will depend, again, on how we define creativity and what we prioritize from it. The environments above might produce more risky or radical innovation, but not necessarily know to appreciate adaptive, evolutionary creativity. The norms and spaces of different cultures will favour different creative processes and outcomes.

This holds true also for creative domains. The sciences and the arts flourished in Europe during the Renaissance (both) and, later, the Enlightenment (science) and Romanticism (art). But many scientific investigations, for example into astronomy and physics, were discouraged during the Middle Ages. And yet the creativity associated with praising God, including through the construction of magnificent cathedrals and places of worship, was highly valued. In India, for instance, creativity in the spiritual domain is fostered by the many religions, festivities, and practices on the Indian subcontinent. This is not necessarily the case today in Western societies, which are mostly secular. In exchange, creativity in the technological domain and artificial intelligence is promoted worldwide, East and West alike.

Besides the encouragement (and discouragement) of creative activities in particular domains and fields of activity, the broader cultural context shapes everyday spaces such as the home, the school, the workplace, and, more generally, the public sphere. In the case of children, focusing on what is specific for creative expression at home versus at the school helps us understand more than children's lives: it also reveals something interesting about creativity and space. Different life contexts come with their own physical, social, and (micro)cultural arrangements. These can all be aligned to stimulate creativity—or at least certain forms of creativity—or can include mismatches in what they offer and what they demand. As an example of the former, some children are sent to schools that promote creative forms of education and their schedule at home is also filled with activities meant to stimulate their imagination and creativity. For the latter, we can think of discrepancies between how parents and teachers evaluate creativity and stimulate creative expression.

A new space for creativity has been opened over the past two decades for young people and adults alike through the emergence of social media and meme culture. Online environments in which users can create their own profiles, in the way they wish, and interact with others on an unprecedented scale, continue to transform our understanding of what it means to be creative. From the social media celebrities of today to the use of such platforms in recent protests and revolutions, including the Arab Springs, we can no longer ignore the impact of online, interactive environments on who, how, when, and where we create. There are certainly things to be optimistic about in this regard, including the phenomenon of crowdfunding for creative ideas and initiatives. At the same time, bullying and the wide spread of misinformation and conspiracy theories in online communities proves that malevolent creativity can also be emboldened by the anonymity and reach of the Internet.

Audiences for creativity

The when and where of creativity would not be complete without considering also the role of other people. I call these people 'audiences' in order to capture the fact that they are essential for the creative actor's activity. As mentioned in Chapter 4 under social processes of creativity, we fundamentally create with and for others, with perspective-taking and dialogue with the views of others constantly guiding creative action. Audiences are thus represented by family, friends, collaborators, competitors, critics and, for Big or historical acts of creativity, also the general public. In this section, we will examine more deeply how others can act as a context for creativity and, in doing so, develop it further.

One of the main roles other people play when it comes to creative work is that of evaluators. Whether their evaluation is implicit and indirect (as when a teacher advises some students but not others to continue doing art) or direct and explicit (when a judge in an art competition gives scores and makes comments), it has great impact on one's creative production and the future of one's creative processes. Empirical research has shown, for example, that being observed and evaluated by others while creating can have a negative impact. This is especially the case when evaluations and awards decrease intrinsic motivation (see Chapter 2 for more details) or simply put extra pressure on the creator. But others' feedback can also be constructive and useful and, in many ways, we couldn't even imagine the development of creativity without the help, comments, and guidance of others.

Oftentimes we need to persuade other people about the creative value of our processes and outcomes. These others, in a position of power vis-à-vis the social recognition of creativity, are called gatekeepers. They play an essential role in selecting what gets to be exhibited, awarded, or published in a variety of domains, from art and design to science and invention. Mihaly Csikszentmihalyi famously gave gatekeepers a key place in his systems model of creativity. For him, a complete understanding of this phenomenon could not stop at the individual alone. We need to also take into account different audiences and gatekeepers (the field) and the culture one tries to contribute to (the domain). It is in the dynamic between individuals, social fields, and cultural domains that creativity happens, with the creator trying to convince the field that his or her creations are worthy of the domain.

But there is much more to the social context of creativity than gatekeepers alone. In the end, most of the creative actions we engage in don't contribute to a particular cultural field and don't have recognized judges who can come to evaluate them. Most often, other people are simply there to be shown a creative artefact and make sense of it. Indeed, one essential role others play in creative production relates to meaning making. Especially when the exact uses of an artefact are not clear or can be added to—which is in most situations—audiences are called upon to 'complete' the creative act by offering their interpretation of it. This process of interpretation is inherently creative. It helps both creators and other people to see the creative outcome in a new light and thus renews it for everyone involved.

How else today would we consider old paintings such as *Mona Lisa* creative? They are certainly not new any more, and not entirely original either given the numerous other artefacts that resemble them. There is surely an unparalleled degree of mastery that went into painting *Mona Lisa* and art gatekeepers across centuries appreciated it as highly creative and valuable (including Leonardo da Vinci, who is said to have travelled with and worked on it for many years). What gives this particular painting its enormous creative potential is the fact that it has and continues to inspire generations of viewers who have reinterpreted it across the ages. These creative acts range from imagining the story of *Mona Lisa* to creating online memes that place her in a new historical context, giving it new value.

More than reinterpreting a creative outcome, audiences are often tasked with using it. And, in doing so, they come up with new and meaningful additions to what has been done before. This is the process at the heart of user innovation, one of the most important venues for creativity nowadays. This creativity is also enhanced by the 'do it yourself' (DIY) culture of recent decades. More and more people are interested in making their own food, clothes, tools, music, and household repairs. Using existing artefacts opens up the possibility of change, either intentional or accidental. This is how, for example, users can create unique computer hardware with desired properties, initiate new forms of social media based on existing technology, customize their car in original ways, and create street fashion.

In many ways, the invention of the Post-it note exemplifies user innovation. In 1968, Spencer Silver developed a weak adhesive while working at 3M. He wanted in fact to produce a strong glue, so his creation was seen as a failure and disregarded. However, it was kept and remembered by his colleagues. In 1974 one of them, Arthur Fry, is said to have been faced with a practical problem while singing in the church choir. Arthur wanted to hold bookmarks in his hymnal without destroying the page. That is when he imagined the potential of Spencer's adhesive. Post-it notes were not born then and there, though. It took many more years and input from different audiences (e.g. secretaries) to perfect Arthur's intuition. Today we couldn't imagine work life without the simple Post-it. It all began not with one but multiple creators, many of whom started off as users.

In summary, audiences as well as time and space are part of the context of creativity, a context without which there would be no creativity to talk about. It is not only the case that we need time, space, and other people in order to create, but these contextual elements carry, amplify, and even continue one's creative actions and its artefacts. What we should avoid, though, is thinking that there are special times, places, and audiences dedicated for this task and that we should wait for them in order to create something (e.g. we should hold on to our ideas until the brainstorming session starts, until we reach the coffee break room or meet a particular colleague). These elements of the 'when' and 'where' are ever-present so we can always creatively engage them in the here and now. The remaining question is why.

Chapter 6
The why of creativity

I have raised so far a series of questions concerning creativity, each one focused on a specific dimension of it: who (the creative person), what (the creative product), how (the creative process), and when/where (the context and its role). But an equally important question is why we engage in creativity to begin with. Why do we talk so much about this phenomenon? Put simply, why are you reading this Very Short Introduction right now?

The 'why' of creativity can be answered at different levels. On the one hand, we can refer here to what motivates creative people to do what they do. This leads us, as we shall see, to a complex picture of how creators choose their domain and decide what to do and when. On the other hand, this question addresses a deeper level, that of how societies today are built and how they, in turn, construct the meaning and value of creativity. It is this underlying set of assumptions that we should focus on first as it reveals something important not only about creativity, but also about the worlds we live in.

As noted in Chapter 1, our conception of creativity is largely a Western 'invention'. This doesn't mean that people from other geographical and cultural spaces are not creative today or have not been creative through history. A quick look at the achievements of non-Western civilizations in terms of art, science, and discovery—from Persian and Aztec to Carthaginian and Chinese—reveals a very rich and creative cultural production. After all, the alphabet was invented in Phoenicia (modern-day Lebanon) in the second millennium BC, paper in Han Dynasty China in the 2nd century BC and gunpowder during the Tang Dynasty (9th century), and chess in India during the Gupta Empire (AD 280–550). What the West was highly successful at inventing and 'exporting' throughout the world, though, is a view of creativity as central for human and societal development.

This, of course, grew out of a particular history with its unique cultural shifts—from Protestantism and its emphasis on work and wealth, through the Industrial Revolution and Enlightenment, with their focus on science, discovery, and invention, up to today's capitalist, neoliberal societies concerned with relentless production and consumption. Creativity is the thread linking all the above. To create means not to be idle but industrious and hardworking, an agent of your own salvation (see Figure 8). It also leads to mastery over nature, not only over one's own destiny; it fuels progress and wealth driven by invention and acts of discovery. Finally, it helps you generate those things other people want to have, buy, and use.

We talk so much about creativity nowadays and consider it intrinsically valuable largely because of its direct and indirect economic benefits. Students everywhere are trained to be more creative because creativity is a 21st-century skill placed, in 2020, third in the top job market skills by the World Economic Forum. Employers want to cultivate creativity in order for their businesses not only to survive the fast-paced environments of today, but also to thrive and have a competitive advantage over other companies. Politicians claim their policies foster creativity and innovation as preconditions for wealth and indicators of human development. Artists want to be more and more creative in order to win

8. William Hogarth's engraving *Industry and Idleness*, 1747, made during the Enlightenment.

prizes, recognition, and, at the end of the day, some substantial material incentives.

But creativity is not all about money and economy, including in Western societies. There are other (hi)stories out there that help us discover new answers to the question of 'why' creativity. One of these (counter-)narratives invites us to consider the role of creative expression for health and well-being. Donald Winnicott, a psychoanalyst interested in child development, claimed that in early life acts of creative play support psychological health and relate us to other people and to our culture. Ruth Richards, more recently, discussed how everyday forms of creativity—what we called mini or little c creations in Chapter 3—are essential for a person's well-being and harmonious development. The underlying link between mental health and creativity comes from the idea that creative expression is liberating, empowering, and suggests a high degree of psychological safety.

But even this second narrative focuses us almost exclusively on the person of the creator and his or her attributes. If creativity as an economic value is 'measured' in terms of personal wealth, creativity as healthy living and engine of well-being is assessed in terms of personal development. Other people can and do benefit from one's creative expression but only indirectly—they might get rich as well or enjoy having a healthier partner, parent, or colleague. What about the impact of creativity on living together, on maintaining and transforming society? We never create alone, as argued throughout this book, but does this mean that we create for other people? This is almost always the case. Creative actions are a form of communication with other people, acts that convey a message and establish a relationship. Our own creative expression can and does foster the creativity of others, if nothing else by setting a personal example for them. And these other people communicate 'back' to us, adding their own creativity to a dialogue that makes up social life.

At a much deeper level, creativity relates to meaning in life. James C. Kaufman discussed this issue at length, showing that creative work can make life more meaningful and worth living. He argued that many of the issues that give our existence value and meaning, such as the needs for coherence, significance, purpose, and the desire for symbolic immortality, are all related to creativity. He emphasized in particular the temporal dimension of this interplay. Reflecting on one's life course can help us understand where we are and where we are going. Living in the present, creatively, opens us up to the joy of being and of sharing our existence with others. Thinking about the future makes us aware of the fact that our creative outcomes are ultimately our legacy and connection to subsequent generations.

In the end, meaning-making processes themselves are intrinsically creative. We have the freedom to interpret ourselves and the world we live in in a variety of ways, even if we aren't always aware of this possibility. As human beings, we are not only creators of tools, objects, or economic value but of meanings, stories, and different versions of the world. It is this inherent potential to look at reality in a new way and act on it 'as if' it was different that connects creativity with both personal and social change.

And it is this transformative power of creativity that makes it so important for our species, for each and every individual, and for the societies we live in. Its ultimate function is to re-present reality in ways that make it possible to change it or, at least, imagine how it could be changed. This allows us to live, at the same time, within worlds of the 'here and now', of immediate experience, and of the 'then and there', far away times and places, spaces of the '(not) yet here' of imagination and possibility. Through creativity, we imagine the impossible only to make the necessary steps to push back against it.

One last question to raise in a chapter dedicated to the 'why' of creativity is to inquire into whether this phenomenon is good, if it benefits us. From what I have outlined above, it would seem that creative processes always lead to having more and doing things better. They can help us become rich and famous or, at the very least, live normal, healthy lives. They can also open us to the experience of others and make us able to communicate our own experience to them. Last but not least, creating gives meaning to our life, helping us understand our past, cope with the present, and shape our future.

And yet, for each positive 'use' of creativity there may be negative consequences, intentional or unintentional. Creating wealth and economic growth often implies the creative destruction of the old and, with it, of the environment and of the livelihood of many communities around the world. One can gain personal well-being without being concerned at all with the well-being of others. Even the meaning we create about our life might involve looking down upon, discriminating against, or exploiting other people. Are these all creative processes or outcomes if they benefit the self and harm everyone else?

As we saw in Chapter 4, there is such a thing as malevolent creativity. The evidence reviewed in this chapter will show that, while we shouldn't romanticize creativity and see only its positive outcomes, there are many reasons to be optimistic. Yes, we don't always help others, society, or even ourselves through each and every creative act. But the essence of this phenomenon is still one of open-mindedness and appreciation of difference. While not every creative action is ethical, creativity and morality share more with each other than we might think at first. Before exploring this further, let's start by examining different reasons to create and to study creativity and see what we can learn from them.

Reasons to create

The issue of why exactly people create brings us back to motivation. As discussed in Chapter 2, most of the time our motives to be creative are grouped into the broad categories of intrinsic and extrinsic. The first refers to the things we do for their own sake while the second concerns the external rewards we receive (or punishments we avoid). But this is a rough distinction when it comes to creativity. As noted in that chapter, there are not only many reasons to distinguish in each category, especially the extrinsic one, but oftentimes something can act as an intrinsic and extrinsic motivator at different moments in time. Moreover, there are things like feeling good about what you do that can be, at once, intrinsically and extrinsically motivating. What do we find when we dig below the surface?

Sarah Luria and James C. Kaufman raised this question in a study based on interviews with several professional and Big C creators. They wanted not only to understand what motivates a creative person, but how and when this motivation is developed. The two coined the term 'creative needs' and defined them as the lifelong fusion of values, interests, and passion for creativity in particular domains. Their analysis revealed six such needs: Beauty, Power, Discovery, Communication, Individuality, and Pleasure.

A search for beauty is typically associated with artists. All the arts, one way or another, concern themselves with the aesthetic and its reception through the senses. But there is an element of beauty to be found in other types of work as well, including in science. Great mathematicians, for instance, are likely to have an aesthetic experience when coming across the 'perfect' formula. Indeed, beauty can motivate even the most mundane acts of creativity—from gardening to preparing a delicious hot meal. The same need, after all, made our ancestors add ornaments to their tools or in caves where none were needed in a functional sense.

The desire for power is universally human and creators are not exempt from it. While the notion might have some negative connotations, such as the need to control or dominate others, power also involves liberating oneself from unwanted constraints. Creative people, especially when recognized for their talent and achievements, reach a certain social status that gives them more power over others and over public opinion. This kind of wide social influence can be a direct consequence of their creativity—for example, for performing artists or media celebrities—or an indirect result, especially for creators used to working alone or in isolated labs. How this power is put to use will differ widely (and matter most).

The need to discover new things is also universal, but perhaps most acutely experienced by creators. This creative need involves a desire to explore one's environment, to understand it, and to find new and exciting opportunities within it. This was a prime motivator for explorers, particularly during the Age of Discovery (15th to 17th centuries), and it continues to inspire everyone endowed with curiosity and a sense of possibility. Discoveries can be made in science, art, and most other creative domains. They often involve happy accidents, chance, and serendipity, thus a close collaboration between events and a creator's 'prepared mind'.

The need to communicate is closely related to creativity, which, as I mentioned before, is itself a form of communication. Creative expression means articulating one's thoughts and feelings into an outcome that is either put into words or given a material form. This product is most of the time shared with people who get to interpret, evaluate, use, and recreate it for their own purposes. Being creative gives us not only an opportunity to relate to others, and understand their worldview, but also to give shape to our own. The challenge of communicating it aesthetically and effectively is why creativity is required in the first place.

The need for individuality is a particularly strong one when it comes to being creative, at least in a Western conception of this phenomenon. What creativity helps people do is discover themselves, first and foremost, as unique and different from others. It relates to our sense of self as agentic and singular. It is because our creative outcomes are, by definition, novel and original that they make us believe we are so as well. But this is not a need felt across cultures. More collectivistic societies build another sense of self, one that is interdependent on others. In those cases, acts of creativity might be used to reveal the commonalities between people and reinforce connectedness, community, and tradition.

Last but not least in Luria and Kaufman's typology, there is pleasure. The pursuit of pleasure is one of the oldest and most fundamental human motivations. The Epicureans founded a whole philosophy around this notion in Antiquity and, much closer to our times, Freud postulated the role of the 'pleasure principle' as a key driver of the unconscious. Pleasure is also our main intrinsic motivator. Most people act creatively because they (also) like doing so. Power and discovery, individuality and communication come with their own satisfactions and, as such, pleasure is often an underlying dimension within creative action. And there are also things we do purely or entirely for our pleasure (e.g. our hobbies).

An interesting question is how these needs and motives might vary across creative domains. Is it the case that scientists strive more towards discovery while artists might, for instance, prioritize individuality? A study I was involved in together with a team of colleagues from France came close to answering this question by comparing creative activity across five domains: art, design, science, scriptwriting, and music. What is interesting about its findings here is the pattern of similarities and differences between domains when it comes to 'impulses' for creativity. In art, for example, the primary motivator is the desire to create or make something and also to express oneself. In design, the same need to create was complemented by the need to solve a practical problem. In science, including mathematics and physics, the need to solve problems was also found, together with curiosity, as a prime motivator. For scriptwriters and music composers, it was again the motivation to create and to express oneself, just like for artists, that came to the fore. This doesn't mean that a scientist never experiences the need to express himself or herself, only that such needs are more rarely talked about. In the end, there are some clear regularities in one's reasons to be creative within and between domains and, most certainly, across the life course.

Reasons to study creativity

While it is hopefully clearer, from the previous section, why people would engage in creative action, the reasons why they would dedicate time and effort to studying creativity are not yet transparent. It is easy to assume that, just because being creative comes with a series of benefits—from economic growth to mental health—this should more than justify a scientific interest in the phenomenon. But, in practice, we rarely come to document through empirical research the consequences of creativity; most studies focus on its antecedents (enabling factors) and correlates (associated processes). James C. Kaufman has recently launched a call for fellow creativity scholars to demonstrate why creativity matters, not only argue that it does in general terms. He pointed to the fact that some other attributes, such as conscientiousness, in many ways the opposite of creativity, are proven to help people succeed in life. So what would a new agenda for positive outcomes research look like?

First and foremost, when studying creativity, we are investigating something that, even if not uniquely human, essentially contributes to our humanity. While many species of birds and mammals demonstrate some basic creative behaviours, it is humans alone who developed an understanding of creativity and built societies and cultures around it.

Indeed, being creative captures something fundamental about human agency and the way we relate to our environment not as passive recipients of external influences but as active participants. From an early age, children are encouraged to express themselves creatively in play, drawings, and music for a reason. This is not to be creative for creativity's sake, it is to practise the skills and attitudes that will help them later in life and, on a broader level, to find a place for themselves in a world populated by fellow creative beings. Building a self and an identity are, ultimately, preconditions and key outcomes of our creativity.

The study of creativity also sheds new light on how we understand society. Theories of creativity express a broader, societal worldview and come to reinforce existing beliefs about the relationship between individuals and community. For example, if we conceive of creativity mainly in terms of novelty, originality, and a break with tradition, we are more likely to envision the relation between creators and their society as conflictual. Indeed, the myth of the lone genius is premised on the assumption that highly creative people struggle against the social order and are constantly rejected by it. If, on the other hand, we are to emphasize the meaningfulness and value of creative action, we will probably notice the fact that no creator has ever worked outside of his or her society, even when their position within it was marginal. Creative people use the cultural resources available to them in new and surprising ways while collaborating with like-minded people.

This brings us to a third reason for studying creativity—reaching a better understanding of human collaboration. While initially it might sound counterintuitive, at least for those who believe that creative people work essentially alone, a closer examination of creativity reveals implicit and explicit networks of collaboration across time. If we are to adopt a sociocultural view of this phenomenon, we get to notice the fact that all the artefacts that surround us are, ultimately, the outcomes of co-creation. And it is not only working with others, face to face, that leads to exchanging ideas—today, such exchanges can take place in virtual environments. Moreover, because of the cultural resources at our disposal, we can work with the ideas and perspectives of others long after they are gone. These perspectives are internalized and lead to creative dialogues within the person, not only between people.

Such insights into the nature and role of creativity are useful for rethinking both school and workplace practices. We normally assume that the main aim of education is to convey the knowledge, skills, and mindsets needed to succeed in society and in particular professions. For a creativity researcher, this goal is restrictive. It doesn't take into account, for example, the fact that the jobs we prepare students for today might not exist any more or be radically transformed in just a few years. To educate for the future rather than the present requires an understanding of creativity and the importance of flexibility, anticipation, and improvisation within the curriculum. These skills are vital in an increasing number of professions nowadays, even if many organizations resist change and promote creativity and innovation only on paper. There are reasons for distrusting radical innovators, many of them going back to how we define creativity and what we prioritize from it. Research into the value of different ways of being creative would benefit managers and educators alike.

It is by responding to Kaufman's call for more studies into the positive outcomes of creative expression that we can develop informed, evidence-based policies for both education and organizations. These studies should focus on the entire system of creativity including people, artefacts, processes, and context, otherwise we risk reaching partial, even misleading conclusions. If the emphasis falls only on the personal attributes of the creator, for instance, we end up developing forms of education and work that are suitable for a specific type of creative people without understanding that, as contexts change, so do their needs, interactions, and forms of expression. Equally, if we develop research into creative products and their qualities alone, we don't pay sufficient attention to how these grow out of and contribute to a range of existing artefacts, practices, and institutions.

In the end, one might wonder why we should focus on positive outcomes specifically; aren't the negative ones worthy of our attention as well? The reasons why creativity is a positive phenomenon in our life, the lives of others, and in society, are the topic of the next section.

Reasons to value creativity

Like any other social and psychological process, creativity can be used for good or for evil. As noted in Chapter 4, there are benevolent forms of creativity that aim at improving the lives of others and malevolent forms, engaged in with the purpose of harming them. And there are also many other instances in which the line is blurred and creative outcomes either help and harm at the same time or do so in turn, sometimes across different generations. But the uses of a phenomenon don't necessarily reveal its nature. In order to assess why we should value creativity—and I certainly believe we should—we need to return to an analysis of its fundamental processes and their underpinning.

To start with, creativity involves finding alternatives to existing problems or situations. It requires us to think beyond the here and now of our direct experience and imagine what else might be possible within it. In other words, all acts of creativity, big and small, open us to a multitude of possibilities to evaluate and select from. Creativity thus reveals the world to us as multiple and malleable instead of fixed, given, unchangeable. Even if we don't always get to enact many of the solutions or perspectives we envision, the mere act of conceiving them is transformative. Creating opens up the possible in our lives by making us aware of the fact that, at all times, there is more to think about and to do than we initially imagined. Creativity is, as such, a central possibility-enabling phenomenon.

Besides opening up new possibilities, creative action also opens us to the world of others. It does so through having us work with the ideas and perspectives of other people. We only envision reality as multiple and changeable if we ourselves can take the perspective of other people and experience the world from their position. It is because of the fundamental differences between self and others, in terms of views, life experience, and types of knowledge, that any act of perspective-taking enriches the self. In many ways, thus, creative action builds a bridge between creators and audiences, asking both to take each other's perspective. This type of opening can increase the chances of understanding other people and their circumstances better, becoming more compassionate and tolerant towards them.

Another consequence of being flexible vis-à-vis the world is that, through creativity, we can question the status quo and dominant ideologies. We are often 'trapped', in everyday life, by singular and unitary ways of thinking or doing things. There is much we take for granted about the world around us and how it works. In the case of objects, this can take the form of functional fixedness—considering each object as having only one function, the one it was designed for. What creativity does is challenge all of these assumptions. Throughout the creative process, either intentionally or accidentally, we discover that things can be different and that what most people believe to be true doesn't always hold. There is an element of empowerment and resistance within creative acts, independent of whether they concern reimagining society or the functions of objects we use every day.

In relation to reimagining society, creativity has a special role to play in transforming our communal existence. As argued above, a creative mindset makes us aware of hegemonic, singular views and encourages us to find alternatives and challenge their dominance. This is particularly useful in the social and political sphere where the power of various ideologies turns them invisible: we believe they designate the only way things can be done, the only way reality can and should function. The various crises we are confronted with at a planetary level, from environmental destruction to the rise of nationalism and increased inequality, ask of us not only concrete creative action but also new ways of seeing and understanding the world. The highest mission for creativity, therefore, is to develop new worldviews by no longer taking for granted what we have learned or are constantly told.

All the benefits above invite us to consider the relationship between creativity and ethics at a deeper level. We can accept that some creative people act unethically, prioritizing their own gains and disregarding the life of others, while at the same time reflecting on how creativity enables an ethical position. If one central tenet of ethics is the Kantian imperative of not treating others as means, but recognizing in them our shared humanity, then we need to start from valuing each other as creative, agentic beings. We depend on the creativity of others for our own creative expression: on their ideas, on the artefacts they create, on their unique viewpoint. If we fail to acknowledge and respect this creative potential, we won't only be less creative, but deprive the world of new perspectives from which to (re)imagine it. Cultivating the creativity of others is not a means for something else, it should be an end in and of itself. Without this other-acknowledging ethos of creative action, we diminish both the humanity of others and our own humanity.

With this grand conclusion, we have reached one of the deeper answers to the 'why' of creativity. In the end, the reasons for which we engage in creativity are as diverse as the processes and tools we use to be creative. There are particular motives and needs creative people experience throughout their activity and their life. There are also specific benefits associated with engaging in creativity research, both theoretical and applied. Above all, there are intrinsic reasons why creativity enriches our humanity and is intimately related to our existence as social, agentic, and ethical beings. With these in mind, we can now raise a final question concerning the future of creativity. If the arguments presented here stand, this is also a question about our future more generally.

Chapter 7
Creativity: where to?

The future is, by definition, a domain of creativity. Envisioning what might come to be, selecting what should happen, and then helping this vision materialize are all creative acts performed on a daily basis by individuals, groups, and communities. It is all the more interesting, then, to use these processes in order to imagine the future of creativity itself. What will be the next spheres of our life in which creativity will become indispensable? How will our creativity both contribute and adapt to the fast-paced development of technology? Will we witness the development of new creative processes and activities? How will we study or document these advances and what will we learn from them?

As always, if we want to understand anything about the future, we need to first examine the past. While creativity contributes to accelerated growth and some ruptures in the trajectory of different domains, it remains the case that these always grow out of past achievements and contribute to ongoing developments. The most ground-breaking creative acts never come out of nowhere or materialize from thin air. The electric cars of today might seem like a response to current climate challenges, but they also build on a longer history of technological development starting with the experiments done by Scot Andrew Gordon and American Benjamin Franklin in the 1740s. Plastic surgery also seems like a modern invention, and yet we know, for instance, that reconstructive surgery techniques were being used in India by 800 BC. And even the very recent emergence of augmented reality in virtual spaces had been envisioned in 1901 by L. Frank Baum, an author who first conceived the idea of electronic displays overlaying data onto real life. The World Economic Forum predicts, for 2020, the development of a more humanized version of the Internet, data-driven healthcare, and printable organs. The story of humanity, a story of creativity, goes on.

But what roles exactly will creativity play in society due to these developments? Experts like Giovanni Corazza argue that, with the gradual (and, in some sectors, rapid) replacement of humans with machines, human creativity won't decrease in importance but will become vital for our survival and our dignity. He considers here the evolution from the industrial and then information societies of past centuries to the post-information order of today. More and more human decisions are delegated to algorithms that, for better or worse, make things easier to operate, faster, and more efficient. Of course, the post-information society is not post-human in the sense of predicting the disappearance of our species. But it is a (brave) new world in which creativity is likely to be our most distinguishing feature and asset.

The above might read utopian, but there is always an element of utopia—and dystopia—in how we imagine the future and get inspired by—or afraid of—it. Ultimately, utopias and dystopias are products of creative thinking, situated within their own historical context. If we were to look back, today, at the predictions made by people living at the turn of the 19th century for the year 2000, we would discover many visions of the future that never came to be. Take, for example, the set of postcards created in France in 1899 by artists, including Jean-Marc Côté, on the theme *En L'An 2000* or *In the Year 2000* (Figure 9). They proposed that firefighters will be flying around using batwings, that we will domesticate giant seahorses and use them for underwater transport, or that we will all have aerial wing-flapping hover cars. And yet, some

9. The year 2000, seen from the end of the 19th century.

predictions from more than a century ago did come true, for instance communication via video chatting or the astounding growth of the automotive industry.

Missed predictions are not a sign of a failure on the part of our imagination and creativity. On the contrary, they are possibilities that never got to be enacted. Even if many never will (given that, for instance, we would have to first create giant seahorses before we ever considered riding them), they still serve as points of reference for future acts of creativity and imagination (after all, we do talk more and more about genetic modification and even about resurrecting giant species of animals that once roamed the Earth). What this brief example demonstrates is not so much the difficulty of getting predictions right, but the future-oriented nature of human creativity and its deep and wide-ranging societal implications. The question is: where will this creativity take us next and what will it, itself, look like?

I am not going to speculate here about future creations, perhaps for the year 2100, as exciting as putting together such a list might be. What I will focus on in this final chapter is the second question about the future of creativity and our understanding of it. These reflections will necessarily—even if implicitly—deal with the future of society as well, given that all creativity theories grow out of and come to reinforce a specific form of social, political, and economic organization. But before approaching the 'where to' question for creativity research and practice, it is important to take stock of where we are now.

Together with James C. Kaufman I have recently tackled this question in proposing what we call the Creativity Matrix. This matrix includes on one axis different components of the creativity system and, on the other, different levels of creativity. The first come from my five A's theory which includes actors, audiences, actions, artefacts, and affordances (each one discussed in various chapters in this book). The second is James's and Ron Beghetto's four C model of mini, little, Pro and Big C (if you don't recall it, please revisit Chapter 3).

The matrix essentially identifies a series of conceptual units that could be studied by creativity researchers. For example, if we take the creative actor and consider him or her at four C levels we get to study people's engagement in creative learning (mini c), in small and mundane acts of creativity (little c), in professional creative activities (Pro c) or in historical, revolutionary forms of creativity (Big C). Or, if we take affordances, we can examine how the material environment fosters (or inhibits) each one of these levels of creative expression.

The question James and I raised is which of these conceptual units we know most about, and which ones remain systematically understudied. In other words, what are the spotlights of creativity research and where do we find blind spots (and why)? Unsurprisingly given the information covered in this short book, one of the most intensely studied areas of the Creativity Matrix is represented by the actor–action–artefact triad. This includes research into who, how, and what is being created, discussed in

Chapters 2 to 4. We also know a lot about the intersection between creative actions and affordances at the mini and little c level. What we should focus our attention more on in the future is Pro c and affordances, in other words, how creativity plays out in the case of professionals and what is the role of the material environment in supporting creative expression of different magnitudes.

It is not difficult to understand why these two areas—professionals and affordances—might be in the blind spot. To start with, they are highly domain specific in the sense that they would focus our attention on context rather than deriving universal knowledge about creativity. Second, we need new analytical and methodological tools in order to grasp the materiality of creative action. While creativity researchers are very good at studying ideas and their properties (e.g. fluency, flexibility, originality, elaboration), they are less well equipped when it comes to incorporating the body, tools, and physical spaces in empirical studies. This has largely to do with the difficulty of considering material and social processes alongside—and especially in their interrelation with—psychological ones. There is more to be done when it comes to integrating 'creative thinking' into 'creative doing'. Last but not least, there are also historical reasons why, for example, we tend to focus on the most impactful forms of creativity and on the creative actor rather than his or her audiences.

In this chapter, I will unpack some of these reasons and their associated limitations in launching two calls for creativity research in the 21st century. The first one concerns what I call the democratization of creativity—the effort to be more inclusive in who we identify as creative, expand our view of creative outcomes, and generally increase everyone's participation in creative activities. The second, related call is to socialize creativity, by which I mean to take the role of other people, society, and culture more seriously in our understanding of this phenomenon. Both these aims can be achieved, I will argue at the end, through research that cuts across disciplinary boundaries. An outline of how a multidisciplinary science of creativity would look is offered before concluding.

Democratizing creativity

How easy or hard is it for someone to consider himself or herself creative? This is the core question at the heart of efforts to make creativity a more inclusive concept. As we have repeatedly seen in this book, the potential to engage in creative action is ever-present. There are personality traits like openness to experience and tolerance for ambiguity that predispose us towards creativity. We live in fast-changing worlds, 'populated' by the creations of others that serve as sources of inspiration and motivate us to create. Interacting with other people and taking their perspective always brings us new insights about the world, including about ourselves. Finally, objects have properties we gradually discover and act upon, affording new and surprising actions.

Consequently, given the way we exist as human beings and how our world is made, we are rather 'condemned' to creativity. And yet, many would think twice when asked whether they consider themselves to be creative people. This is primarily because of a certain social construction of creativity as a quality only geniuses or highly eminent persons possess, or a label reserved for those artefacts that radically transform our culture and contribute to history. In other words, what we have called Big C creators and historical creations.

Of course, we all know other discourses, including about everyday life creativity, and we do appreciate people who seem to demonstrate it. For instance, those who are quick to improvise when the situation requires it, who solve mundane problems in new and surprising ways, who enjoy challenges and not knowing the answer to something. We do have, collectively, an understanding of such mini and little c creativity but do we appreciate it, at least in Western societies, as much as historical creativity? Often this is not the case. We focus on the peaks of creative expression, forgetting that every mountain top has a base and this base, in the case of creativity, is represented by the mundane actions of ordinary, creative people, exploring the world and doing so passionately, on a daily basis.

Psychological studies of creativity had a great role to play in democratizing our understanding of this phenomenon. If 19th- and early 20th-century studies focused mainly on eminent creators in science or art, the 1950s brought to our attention mundane forms of creativity. It was because we started thinking of creativity not only as achievement (and, in particular, socially recognized achievements) but also as potential, that we started to see this potential within ourselves and within other people.

There is something problematic, however, in drawing too sharp a distinction between creative potential and creative achievement. This would suggest that there is potential outside of action and that this phenomenon resides somehow in the person. A more dynamic and relational understanding of creative potential would 'locate' it within material actions and ongoing interactions between creators, artefacts, and audiences.

But there is ultimately a lot to be gained from the idea that we are all capable of creative processes and that creativity is malleable and can be educated. While we can never reach a 'formula' for how to make people more creative—indeed, this would go against the very nature of creativity—there are many ways to foster original thinking and actions. These don't concern only the creative person and exercising individual abilities but focus our attention on how we can build environments conducive for creativity. The latter are usually rich in opportunities for trying out things, making mistakes, and being able to learn from them.

If we take seriously the idea that every act of creativity should be appreciated in its own right and that this phenomenon accompanies most person–environment interactions, then why don't we find more examples of creativity in daily life, including in our own activity?

James C. Kaufman and I reflected on this question when we recently proposed the CASE model of shadow or hidden creativities. This framework starts from the simple observation that a lot of our ideas, actions, and artefacts do have some novelty and usefulness. We don't spend our lives thinking, saying, or doing exactly the same things; in fact, this would actually be impossible. And even when the distance between what we create, in the present, and what existed before is significant, we can still be reluctant to call ourselves creative.

We found four reasons—and there certainly can be others—why this might be the case. In the CASE acronym that captures them, C stands for capital, A for awareness, S for the spark, and E for exceptionality. Let's take them in turn.

Many potential creators never get to be recognized for their activity because they lack social and cultural capital. This means that they are missing the right social connections and cultural tools (e.g. enough knowledge of the field or experience within it) to have their creativity acknowledged and promoted. While this doesn't imply that they themselves can't consider their work creative, it is difficult in practice to believe things nobody else believes in or go on doing things that are not recognized by anyone else. Missing cultural capital also means missing the right arguments to defend one's actions and artefacts as creative.

Often a lack of capital is associated with a lack of awareness that what is being done is indeed creative or could be seen as such. We do many things in our everyday life—in how we drive, cook, or interact with others and solve problems—that could be considered creative and yet label these as routine and more of the same. Being aware of one's own creative potential and its expression is a precondition for having it recognized by others.

The spark doesn't refer here to any innate property of the person but to the fact of having been the first to come up with something. A lot of everyday life creativity continues, transforms, and renews what other people have done. Think, for example, about fan fiction or user innovation (for a reminder revisit Chapter 6). Unfortunately, because the person was not the original creator, he or she gets little credit for giving old artefacts a new life.

Finally, exceptionality is a quality added on top of novelty, originality, and value. In everyday life, unlike what the scientific definition says, we don't look only for new and meaningful things, but for things that stand out, grab our attention, and demonstrate high levels of mastery. This is why, for instance, students are rarely seen as being creative—or asked to be creative—because we assume that learning leads to mastery only over time. As such, we don't really expect or are prepared to discover creativity in the work of someone who is learning. It's interesting also to notice here that exceptionality is not a property intrinsic to some artefacts and not others, but a type of value we construct socially and culturally.

Armed with this new understanding, how can we use the CASE model to democratize creativity? First of all, by paying attention to where capital, awareness, the initial spark, and exceptionality are missing and still keeping an open mind about the creativity of the people, processes, and products involved. Second, by helping potential creators to develop those resources they lack to have their work more widely recognized. For example, we can help a talented writer get in touch with an agent (social capital) or guide a young person to those schools that would best develop their creative potential (exceptionality).

After all, the issue of whether something should be appreciated or not as (potentially) creative reminds us of Pascal's wager about the existence of God. He logically demonstrated that we are better off believing in God in all cases, even if God turns out not to exist. Something similar can be said about creativity. What do we lose from trying to discover creativity in something that turns out not to have creative value after all? We might use some time and energy but perhaps open the mind of someone to the idea that they could indeed be creative. Conversely, what is the cost of not appreciating creativity that is clearly there? People get discouraged and stop doing creative things, a decision that comes at a personal cost and that ultimately makes all of us live in creativity-impoverished societies.

Socializing creativity

As the history of creativity studies demonstrates, democratizing this phenomenon is not the same as socializing it. Psychologists have been studying, since the 1950s, the creative potential of each and every person, but each person taken separately. We can all be creative and are creative, one way or another, but this is because of our intelligence, motivation, and personality traits. The environment, including other people around us, can only enhance or diminish our individual creative potential. To socialize creativity, we need to recognize the fact that other people are not simply external influences or conditions for our creative expression. They are part and parcel of what we call individual creativity.

We need a major shift within creativity research and, in many ways, in the way societies recognize achievement, in order to acknowledge the relational and distributed nature of creative processes. In research, we would need to develop conceptual and methodological tools able not only to capture the bidirectional interactions between person and world but to depict the two as interdependent. For instance, notions like perspective and affordance. These are relations rather than intra-individual variables. Perspectives relate person and world by capturing the action orientation of an individual. Affordances are action potentials defined, at once, by the properties of objects and those of the person. A new affordance is noticed when the individual adopts the perspective that makes it 'visible', for example a water bottle can serve as a paper weight but only when we are looking for something heavy.

At a societal level, the challenge is to appreciate group creativity and acts of co-creation. We know that all the creative artefacts surrounding us necessarily came about due to the work of several people (even if only one might have had the initial idea for them), but still evaluate creativity as if it was an individual affair. A quick look at the way prizes are offered or monuments are being erected reveals our cultural bias towards singular creators. These are all part of the political economy of creativity and the broader question of which ideas and inventions we collectively regard as valuable and worthy of recognition (and protection) in society, and which ones are free to be used by everyone. For example, in the Western world, creative outcomes that emerge from the traditions of entire communities, such as indigenous people, have often been considered free for personal use. In contrast, individual artists', designers', or scientists' work is almost automatically protected by law.

Copyright laws make individualizing tendencies even more obvious. They are meant to protect the rights of the person or people who author a given, valuable artefact. The latter are not necessarily single individuals, even if these are the typical copyright holders. But the principle on which copyright laws are currently built generates a sharp distinction between creators and their collaborators, users, and followers. It isn't only the case that often this line is hard to draw, but the creativity of other people who might otherwise benefit from the new and valuable artefact and re-create it for their own purposes is considerably restricted.

Does this mean that socializing creativity is equivalent to denying the role and importance of the individual? Certainly not. This is not a call to disregard or diminish personal creative expression; it is one to recognize this expression at once as personal and social. It is not an anti-individual approach, but an anti-individualistic and anti-reductionist one. Focusing only on the person's creative contribution, taken out of context, is both partial and misleading. As argued here (see Chapter 5), context is part of the phenomenon when it comes to creativity. Its acknowledgement doesn't make us underestimate the role of the person but understand it more fully. It is because each creator is part of a network of people, objects, places, and institutions that he or she can develop a unique way of thinking, seeing, and doing things. Our social nature doesn't contradict our individuality, it constitutes its very basis. It is because, not in spite, of others that we create and do so in uniquely human ways.

Towards a multidisciplinary science of creativity

A participatory and social model of creativity, argued for above, can only be achieved through the means of a multidisciplinary approach. Creativity research has been, for the past seven decades, dominated by psychologists. Like any discipline, psychology has its own strengths and limitations. When it comes to this area of study, psychological research has helped us understand creative potential in much more 'democratic' terms while remaining focused on individual-level processes. We need inputs from other disciplines, including sociology, anthropology, and history, to achieve the socialization mentioned before. And there is much more to individual level processes that we can consider, beyond psychology. Biology and neuroscience help us understand creativity, for instance, as embodied action.

Before unpacking further these different contributions, a brief note on the difference between inter-, multi-, and transdisciplinary approaches. There is widespread agreement nowadays that, for examining complex phenomena, situations, and events, we need to move beyond disciplinary perspectives. This is because no single discipline can offer us a comprehensive view of a multifaceted object of study or respond to the challenge of cultivating it in practice. Creativity is certainly a case in point. Psychological studies illuminate the cognitive (sometimes also the emotional and motivational) dynamic of creativity, yet they are largely silent when it comes to social and material processes.

What is important is how we consider disciplinary approaches and what kind of dialogues we establish between them. Interdisciplinarity calls for complementing a given point of view with new perspectives without changing any of them. An interdisciplinary study of creativity would thus present, side by side, what a sociologist, anthropologist, or educator might have to say about creative people and processes. What we learn from this exercise is limited by the fact that we don't actually get to combine or adapt the different approaches. This is the task of multidisciplinarity—an effort to consider one disciplinary perspective through the lens of another and adjust these perspectives to each other. For instance, when a sociologist and a psychologist exchange views about creativity, the resulting approach shares some characteristics from each discipline and some new features that came out of the dialogue. Transdisciplinarity goes a step further by aiming to transcend disciplines altogether. In this scenario, the researchers involved would avoid thinking 'like' a sociologist or psychologist and apply any kind of useful knowledge to the problem at hand. The danger here is that doing away with disciplines marks also the end of expertise.

This is why, in my view, a multidisciplinary theory of creativity is what the field should aim for. The problem is not having disciplinary approaches; indeed, there are many reasons why it's good to learn specific ways of thinking and doing research. The challenge is dialogue and being able to learn from other people with other ways of thinking and doing things.

In the Creativity Matrix I discussed at the beginning of this chapter, James and I considered also how different disciplines help us understand different parts of the network. For instance, the creative actor can be studied from the perspective of psychology, education, business, and neuroscience. Affordances, however, are mainly studied in design, engineering, and business. Mini c is primarily the realm of psychology, education, aesthetics, and, to some extent, design, while Big C is studied by psychologists, business experts, and engineers. A key accomplishment of a multidisciplinary theory would be to learn from each one of these fields (and more) and be able to integrate their insights into unitary wholes.

Let's take a concrete example of this. Audiences or the role of other people in creativity can be approached from different disciplinary perspectives. Psychologists consider the impact the actual or imagined presence of others might have on creative expression. Business scholars think of audiences as users, evaluators, or adaptors of existing innovations. Educators are likely to consider the formative role interacting with others can have on the creative person through guidance, feedback, and modelling behaviour. Designers might be concerned by how audiences perceive (or not) affordances or possibilities to use a given artefact in a specific way. Sociologists call our attention to the fact that others are represented not only by people but also by gatekeepers and institutions. Anthropologists make us aware that cultural norms influence who gets to judge what is creative and how. Philosophers will tell us that the notions of others and otherness have a long history and what matters is the kind of intersubjective relations involved in them.

A dialogue between these different—sometimes radically different—perspectives would go a long way in terms of what I call here the socialization of creativity. It would show, first of all, that the notion of audience has multiple meanings and that there are various theories available to study audiences as users (design), collaborators (psychology), gatekeepers (sociology), or role models (education). More than this, these perspectives can and should enrich each other. A philosopher's reflection on how we sometimes marginalize or fear other people should help psychologists consider their implicit assumptions and experimental designs which systematically favour individual over groupwork. An educational point of view can be merged with a sociological one in order to understand how institutions enable creativity or, at the very least, act as channels for specific types of creative expression. Finally, a design approach could take creativity studies further—as it has through the emergence and spread of design thinking—by illuminating how solving problems creatively requires taking the perspective of present and future users. How exactly these perspectives are taken, exchanged, or rejected is, itself, a psychological topic.

When we raise thus the question of 'where to' for creativity, we cannot think any more in terms of single disciplines and domains. Multidisciplinary collaborations are taking place as I am writing this final chapter. The democratization of creativity continues through such work and its socialization is slowly but surely under way.

A new era of connectivity, networks, and globalization depends on creative action and also shapes it, including our theories of the creative person, product, and process. In many ways, this is the time when we need creativity more than ever before. Faced with a rapidly deteriorating climate, economies weakened by COVID-19, and the rise of populism and nationalism, we cannot assume that old solutions will continue to apply. But, before throwing out the baby with the bath water, we should also think about what kind of creativity we want to encourage. Is it the radical, breakthrough innovation of 'move fast and break things'? Or, surrounded by so many broken things—including our shattered sense of truth and trust in one another—would we be better off adopting incremental, adaptive change?

No matter which way we go, we will be well served by understanding the nature, processes, and consequences of our creativity. This Very Short Introduction marks the beginning of a journey which has to do with much more than creativity itself. I hope to have convinced you that, as we study this phenomenon, we actually get to discover a lot about ourselves and the kind of societies we live in. And, hopefully, also something about the future. If we are 'condemned' to create, then we are also condemned to always look ahead. It is through creativity that we bring the future into the present, a power that carries with it plenty of joy and excitement, an acute sense of possibility, as well as some important responsibilities.

References and further reading

Chapter 1: Creativity: what is it?

Those interested in the history of creativity are invited to read:

Glăveanu, V. P. & Kaufman, J. C. (2019). Creativity: A historical perspective. In J. C. Kaufman & R. Sternberg (Eds), *The Cambridge handbook of creativity*, 2nd edition (pp. 9–26). Cambridge: Cambridge University Press.

Hanson, M. H. (2015). *Worldmaking: Psychology and the ideology of creativity*. London: Springer.

Mason, J. H. (2003). *The value of creativity: An essay on intellectual history, from Genesis to Nietzsche*. Aldershot: Ashgate.

Weiner, R. P. (2000). *Creativity and beyond: Cultures, values, and change*. Albany, NY: State University of New York Press.

For more information about the paradigms of creativity see:

Glăveanu, V. P. (2010). Paradigms in the study of creativity: Introducing the perspective of cultural psychology. *New Ideas in Psychology*, 28(1), 79–93.

For different definitions of creativity do check the following sources:

Csikszentmihalyi, M. (1988). Society, culture, and person: A systems view of creativity. In R. Sternberg (Ed.), *The nature of creativity: Contemporary psychological perspectives* (pp. 325–39). Cambridge: Cambridge University Press.

Glăveanu, V. P. (2015). Creativity as a sociocultural act. *Journal of Creative Behavior*, 49(3), 165–80.

Stein, M. (1953). Creativity and culture. *Journal of Psychology*, *36*, 311–22.

Weisberg, R. (1993). *Creativity: Beyond the myth of the genius*. New York: W. H. Freeman and Co.

Finally, for agency, imagination, improvisation, and innovation you can consult the following:

Anderson, N., Potočnik, K., & Zhou, J. (2014). Innovation and creativity in organizations: A state-of-the-science review, prospective commentary, and guiding framework. *Journal of Management, 40*(5), 1297–333.

Emirbayer, M., & Mische, A. (1998). What is agency? *American Journal of Sociology*, *103*(4), 962–1023.

Hallam, E., & Ingold, T. (Eds) (2007). *Creativity and cultural improvisation*. Oxford: Berg.

Zittoun, T., & Gillespie, A. (2015). *Imagination in human and cultural development*. London: Routledge.

Chapter 2: The who of creativity

For more details about creativity and intelligence, you are invited to consult:

Gardner, H. (1993). *Creating minds: An anatomy of creativity seen through the lives of Freud, Einstein, Picasso, Stravinsky, Eliot, Graham, and Gandhi*. New York: Basic Books.

Karwowski, M., Dul, J., Gralewski, J., Jauk, E., Jankowska, D. M., Gajda, A.,...& Benedek, M. (2016). Is creativity without intelligence possible? A necessary condition analysis. *Intelligence*, *57*, 105–17.

Sternberg, R. J. (2003). *Wisdom, intelligence, and creativity synthesized*. New York: Cambridge University Press.

For more information about creativity and personality, see:

Feist, G. J. (1998). A meta-analysis of personality in scientific and artistic creativity. *Personality and Social Psychology Review*, *2*(4), 290–309.

McCrae, R. R. (1987). Creativity, divergent thinking, and openness to experience. *Journal of Personality and Social Psychology*, *52*(6), 1258.

Puryear, J. S., Kettler, T., & Rinn, A. N. (2019). Relating personality and creativity: Considering what and how we measure. *The Journal of Creative Behavior*, *53*(2), 232–45.

For creativity and motivation, consider the following:

Amabile, T. M. (1996). *Creativity in context: Update to the social psychology of creativity*. Boulder, CO: Westview Press.

Dweck, C. S. (2008). *Mindset: The new psychology of success*. New York: Random House.

Karwowski, M., & Kaufman, J. C. (Eds). (2017). *The creative self: Effect of beliefs, self-efficacy, mindset, and identity*. London: Academic Press.

Last but not least, for a highly enjoyable read about outsider art, *art brut*, and creativity, see:

Maclagan, D. (2010). *Outsider art: From the margins to the marketplace*. London: Reaktion Books.

Chapter 3: The what of creativity

For the creativity of ideas, objects, and the life course you are advised to consult:

Glăveanu, V. P. (2011). Creating creativity: Reflections from fieldwork. *Integrative Psychological and Behavioral Science*, *45*(1), 100–15.

Runco, M. A., & Acar, S. (2012). Divergent thinking as an indicator of creative potential. *Creativity Research Journal*, *24*(1), 66–75.

Zittoun, T., & de Saint-Laurent, C. (2015). Life-creativity: Imagining one's life. In V. Glăveanu, A. Gillespie, & J. Valsiner (Eds), *Rethinking creativity: Contributions from cultural psychology* (pp. 58–75). London: Routledge.

For levels of creativity and types of creative contributions, read the following:

Boden, M. (1994). What is creativity? In M. Boden (Ed.), *Dimensions of creativity* (pp. 75–117). London: MIT Press/Bradford Books.

Kaufman, J. C., & Beghetto, R. A. (2009). Beyond big and little: The four C model of creativity. *Review of General Psychology*, *13*(1), 1–12.

Kaufman, J. C., & Glăveanu, V. P. (in press). Making the CASE for Shadow Creativity. *Psychology of Aesthetics, Creativity, and the Arts*.

Sternberg, R. J., Kaufman, J. C., & Pretz, J. E. (2002). *The creativity conundrum*. Philadelphia: Psychology Press.

For malevolent forms of creativity, the dynamic definition and exaptation, these are a few good sources:

Andriani, P., Ali, A., & Mastrogiorgio, M. (2017). Measuring exaptation and its impact on innovation, search, and problem solving. *Organization Science*, 28(2), 320–38.

Corazza, G. E. (2016). Potential originality and effectiveness: The dynamic definition of creativity. *Creativity Research Journal*, 28(3), 258–67.

Cropley, D. H., Cropley, A. J., Kaufman, J. C., & Runco, M. A. (Eds). (2010). *The dark side of creativity*. New York: Cambridge University Press.

Sierra, Z., & Fallon, G. (2016). Rethinking creativity from the 'South': Alternative horizons toward strengthening community-based well-being. In V. P. Glăveanu (Ed.), *The Palgrave handbook of creativity and culture research* (pp. 355–74). London: Palgrave Macmillan.

Last but not least, for more information on Golden Ages and creativity, see:

Simonton, D. K. (2018). Intellectual genius in the Islamic Golden Age: Cross-civilization replications, extensions, and modifications. *Psychology of Aesthetics, Creativity, and the Arts*, 12(2), 125–35.

Chapter 4: The how of creativity

For more information about the psychological processes of creativity consult:

Finke, R. A., Ward, T. B., & Smith, S. M. (1992). *Creative cognition: Theory, research and applications*. Cambridge, MA: MIT Press.

Lubart, T. I. (2001). Models of the creative process: Past, present and future. *Creativity Research Journal*, 13(3–4), 295–308.

Simonton, D. K. (2011). Creativity and discovery as blind variation: Campbell's (1960) BVSR model after the half-century mark. *Review of General Psychology*, 15(2), 158–74.

For details about the social processes of creativity see:

Glăveanu, V. P. (2015). Creativity as a sociocultural act. *Journal of Creative Behavior*, 49(3), 165–80.

Osborn, A. F. (1957). *Applied imagination* (revised edition). New York: Scribner.

Reiter-Palmon, R. (Ed.). (2017). *Team creativity and innovation.* New York: Oxford University Press.

For material processes of creativity, you are invited to read the following:

Bevan, B., Petrich, M., & Wilkinson, K. (2014). Tinkering is serious play. *Educational Leadership,* 72(4), 28–33.

Gibson, J. J. (1966). *The senses considered as perceptual systems.* Boston, MA: Houghton Mifflin.

Glăveanu, V. P. (2012). What can be done with an egg? Creativity, material objects and the theory of affordances. *Journal of Creative Behavior,* 46(3), 192–208.

More generally, for the creative process and creativity as action, consider the following:

Glăveanu, V. P. (2012). Habitual creativity: Revisiting habit, reconceptualising creativity. *Review of General Psychology,* 16(1), 78–92.

Wallas, G. (1926). *The art of thought.* London: J. Cape.

And for the creativity of Easter eggs, if you are ever curious about it, see this article:

Glăveanu, V. P. (2013). Creativity and folk art: A study of creative action in traditional craft. *Psychology of Aesthetics, Creativity, and the Arts,* 7(2), 140–54.

Chapter 5: The when and where of creativity

For more information about creativity and time, check the following sources:

Festinger, L. (1983). *The human legacy.* New York: Columbia University Press.

Sawyer, R. K., Csikszentmihalyi, M., John-Steiner, V., Moran, S., Feldman, D. H., Gardner, H., Sternberg, R. J., & Nakamura, J. (2003), *Creativity and development.* New York: Oxford University Press.

Wallace, D. B. (1991). The genesis and microgenesis of sudden insight in the creation of literature. *Creativity Research Journal,* 4(1), 41–50.

For details about creativity and space, consult the following:

de Saint Laurent, C., Glăveanu, V. P., & Chaudet, C. (2020). Malevolent creativity and social media: Creating anti-immigration communities on Twitter. *Creativity Research Journal*, online first.

Dul, J., & Ceylan, C. (2011). Work environments for employee creativity. *Ergonomics*, *54*(1), 12–20.

Hofstede, G. (2001). *Culture's consequences: Comparing values, behaviors, institutions, and organizations across nations* (2nd edition). Thousand Oaks, CA: Sage.

Finally, for more on creativity and the role of audiences, here are some valuable sources:

Csikszentmihalyi, M. (2014). Society, culture, and person: A systems view of creativity. In M. Csikszentmihalyi (Ed.), *The systems model of creativity* (pp. 47–61). Dordrecht: Springer.

Glăveanu, V. P. (2014). *Distributed creativity: Thinking outside the box of the creative individual*. Cham: Springer.

Von Hippel, E. (2005). Democratizing innovation: The evolving phenomenon of user innovation. *Journal für Betriebswirtschaft*, *55*(1), 63–78.

Last but not least, for the Amusement Park Theory of creativity and the domain generality and domain specificity debate consider the following:

Baer, J. (1998). The case for domain specificity of creativity. *Creativity Research Journal*, *11*, 173–7.

Kaufman, J. C., & Baer, J. (2005). The Amusement Park Theory of creativity. In J. C. Kaufman & J. Baer (Eds), *Creativity across domains: Faces of the muse* (pp. 321–8). Mahwah, NJ: Erlbaum.

Plucker, J. A. (1998). Beware of simple conclusions: The case for content generality of creativity. *Creativity Research Journal*, *11*, 179–82.

Chapter 6: The why of creativity

For the relation between creativity and development, mental health, and meaning in life, read the following sources:

Kaufman, J. C. (2018). Finding meaning with creativity in the past, present, and future. *Perspectives on Psychological Science*, *13*(6), 734–49.

Richards, R. (2018). *Everyday creativity and the healthy mind: Dynamic new paths for self and society*. London: Palgrave.

Winnicott, D. W. (1971). *Playing and reality*. London: Tavistock.

For reasons why people engage in creativity consider the following sources:

Glăveanu, V. P., Lubart, T., Bonnardel, N., Botella, M., de Biaisi, M.-P., Desainte-Catherine, M., Georgsdottir, A., Guillou, K., Kurtag, G., Mouchiroud, C., Storme, M., Wojtczuk, A., & Zenasni, F. (2013). Creativity as action: Findings from five creative domains. *Frontiers in Educational Psychology*, *4*, 1–14.

Hennessey, B. A. (2010). The creativity–motivation connection. In J. C. Kaufman & R. J. Sternberg (Eds), *The Cambridge handbook of creativity* (pp. 342–65). New York: Cambridge University Press.

Luria, S. R., & Kaufman, J. C. (2017). The dynamic force before intrinsic motivation: Exploring creative needs. In M. Karwowski & J. C. Kaufman (Eds), *The creative self: How our beliefs, self-efficacy, mindset, and identity impact our creativity* (pp. 318–23). San Diego, CA: Academic Press.

For reasons to study creativity, review the following:

Glăveanu, V. P. (2018). Creativity in and for society. *Creativity. Theories–Research–Applications*, *5*(2), 155–8.

Kaufman, J. C. (2018). Creativity's need for relevance in research and real life: Let's set a new agenda for positive outcomes. *Creativity. Theories–Research–Applications*, *5*(2), 124–37.

Sternberg, R. J. (2018). Yes, creativity can predict academic success! *Creativity. Theories–Research–Applications*, *5*(2), 142–5.

Last but not least, for the reasons we should value creativity, consider the following:

Glăveanu, V. P. (2018). The possible as a field of inquiry. *Europe's Journal of Psychology*, *14*(3), 519.

Groyecka, A. (2018). Will becoming more creative make us more tolerant? *Creativity. Theories–Research–Applications*, *5*(2), 170–6.

Moran, S., Cropley, D., & Kaufman, J. (Eds) (2014). *The ethics of creativity*. London: Palgrave.

Chapter 7: Creativity: where to?

For more information about the Creativity Matrix, read the following paper:

Glăveanu, V. P. & Kaufman, J. C. (2019). The Creativity Matrix: Spotlights and blind spots in our understanding of the phenomenon. *Journal of Creative Behavior*, early view.

For efforts to democratize creativity, consider the following:

Craft, A. (2001). Little c creativity. In A. Craft, B. Jeffrey, & M. Leibling (Eds), *Creativity in Education* (pp. 45–61). London: Continuum.

Guilford, J. P. (1967). Creativity: Yesterday, today and tomorrow. *The Journal of Creative Behavior*, *1*(1), 3–14.

Kaufman, J. C., & Glăveanu, V. P. (in press). Making the CASE for Shadow Creativity. *Psychology of Aesthetics, Creativity, and the Arts*.

For socializing creativity, here are a few sources:

Hennessey, B. A. (2003). The social psychology of creativity. *Scandinavian Journal of Educational Research*, *47*(3), 253–71.

Montuori, A., & Purser, R. E. (1995). Deconstructing the lone genius myth: Toward a contextual view of creativity. *Journal of Humanistic Psychology*, *35*(3), 69–112.

Simonton, D. K. (1975). Sociocultural context of individual creativity: A transhistorical time-series analysis. *Journal of Personality and Social Psychology*, *32*(6), 1119.

For the disciplinary, inter-, and multidisciplinary study of creativity, consider the following:

Gardner, H. (1988). Creativity: An interdisciplinary perspective. *Creativity Research Journal*, *1*(1), 8–26.

Kaufman, J. C., Glăveanu, V. P., & Baer, J. (Eds) (2017). *The Cambridge handbook of creativity across domains*. Cambridge: Cambridge University Press.

Magyari-Beck, I. (1994). Creatology: A postpsychological study. *Creativity Research Journal*, *7*(2), 183–92.

Finally, for a critical (and constructive) reading of creativity studies, see:

Glăveanu, V. P. (2014). The psychology of creativity: A critical reading. *Creativity: Theories–Research–Applications*, *1*(1), 10–32.

Index

For the benefit of digital users, indexed terms that span two pages (e.g., 52–53) may, on occasion, appear on only one of those pages.